OCCASIONAL PAPER 200

Pension Reform in the Baltics
Issues and Prospects

Jerald Schiff, Niko Hobdari, Axel Schimmelpfennig, and Roman Zytek

INTERNATIONAL MONETARY FUND
Washington DC
2000

© 2000 International Monetary Fund

Production: IMF Graphics Section
Figures: Sanaa Elaroussi
Typesetting: Alicia Etchebarne-Bourdin

Cataloging-in-Publication Data

Pension reform in the Baltics: issues and prospects/by Jerald Schiff . . . [et al.].

   p. cm.—(Occasional paper; 200)
   Includes bibliographical references.
   ISBN 1-55775-968-5

   1. Pensions—Baltic States. 2. Baltic States—Social policy. I. Schiff, Jerald Alan. II. Occasional paper (International Monetary Fund); 200.

HD7197.75 .P46 2000

331.25'2'09479—dc21   00-066082

Price: US$20.00
(US$17.50 to full-time faculty members and
students at universities and colleges)

Please send orders to:
International Monetary Fund, Publication Services
700 19th Street, N.W., Washington, D.C. 20431, U.S.A.
Tel.: (202) 623-7430   Telefax: (202) 623-7201
E-mail: publications@imf.org
Internet: http://www.imf.org

recycled paper

Contents

Preface		v
I	**Overview**	1
II	**Reform of the Pay-As-You-Go Pension Systems**	3
	PAYG in Early Transition Years	3
	Reforming the PAYG System	4
	Experience with Reforms to Date	18
III	**Introduction of a Three-Pillar Pension System**	19
	Introduction of a Three-Pillar System: Pros and Cons	19
	Options for Fully Funded Pillars in the Baltic Countries	23
IV	**Macroeconomic Issues and Program Design**	28
	Pension System Reform and the Savings-Investment Balance	28
	Implications of Pension Reform for Macroeconomic Policy Design	30
V	**Conclusions**	32
References		34
Appendix. Estonia: Pension Reform		35

Boxes

2.1. The Pension Systems at Independence	4
2.2. Latvia: The 1999 Pension Amendments	17
3.1. The World Bank Pension Model	21
3.2. Intergenerational Transfers: Who Pays for the Pensions?	21
3.3. Have Fully Funded Pension System Reforms Lived Up to Expectations?	22
3.4. Alternative Solutions to the Social Security Crisis	23

Tables

2.1. The Baltic States: Household Wealth Held in Bank Deposits	5
2.2. The Baltic States: Impact of Economic Crisis on the Number of Pensioners	6
2.3. Estonia: Financial Performance of the Social Insurance Fund	7
2.4. Latvia: Financial Performance of the Social Fund	8
2.5. Lithuania: Financial Performance of the SoDra	9
2.6. Estonia: Pension Indicators	10
2.7. Latvia: Pension Indicators	11
2.8. Lithuania: Pension Indicators	12

3.1. The Baltic States: Demographic Projections and Theoretical
     Burden of the Pay-As-You-Go Pension System   20
3.2. Latvia: Retirement Scenarios in a Fully Funded System   24
4.1. The Macroeconomic Impact of Pension Reform   31

Figures

2.1. Population Distribution by Age in 1990 and Projected for 2040   13
2.2. Estonia Demographic Projections, 1999–2040   14
2.3. Latvia Demographic Projections, 1990–2040   15
2.4. Lithuania Demographic Projections, 1990–2040   16

Appendix Figures

A.1. Estonia: Demographic Dependency Rates, 1999–2075   37
A.2. Estonia: Surpluses and Replacement Rates of the First Pillar Under
     Alternative Scenarios, 1999–2075   38

The following symbols have been used throughout this paper:

...   to indicate that data are not available;

—   to indicate that the figure is zero or less than half the final digit shown, or that the item does not exist;

–   between years or months (e.g., 1998–99 or January–June) to indicate the years or months covered, including the beginning and ending years or months;

/   between years (e.g., 1998/99) to indicate a fiscal (financial) year.

"Billion" means a thousand million.

Minor discrepancies between constituent figures and totals are due to rounding.

The term "country," as used in this paper, does not in all cases refer to a territorial entity that is a state as understood by international law and practice; the term also covers some territorial entities that are not states, but for which statistical data are maintained and provided internationally on a separate and independent basis.

Preface

This occasional paper provides an overview of efforts in the Baltic countries to reform their pension systems, and examines the choices facing these countries in their continued reform efforts. Early reforms were aimed at correcting the flaws of the inherited Soviet system and, in particular, at shoring up the finances of the pension systems and reducing their distortionary impact. While these policies were largely successful, they have also been partially undone in subsequent years. More recently, all three countries—and many others throughout the world—have turned their attention to addressing adverse demographic trends, by moving toward a three-pillar pension system incorporating a fully funded scheme. The paper emphasizes that while such pension reforms can have significant benefits, they also impose costs and, in any case, do not allow countries to "escape" demographics.

The paper is the product of a team effort of the Baltic Division of the European II Department. In particular, Peter Keller suggested the research topic and played an important role, along with Mr. Schiff, in guiding the project. A number of people, including Günther Taube, Basil Zavoico, Johannes Mueller, Vitali Kramarenko, and Joannes Mongardini provided the necessary data for their countries, and offered helpful suggestions. Insightful comments were provided as well by John Odling-Smee, Gérard Bélanger, Oleh Havrylyshyn, Richard Hemming, and Sanjeev Gupta. Alexandra Merlino provided excellent research assistance, and Jean Boyd and Lilian Immers provided careful and patient secretarial help. Jeremy Clift of the External Relations Department edited the paper and coordinated its production for publication.

The views expressed are solely those of the authors and do not necessarily reflect the views of the IMF, Executive Directors, or the authorities of the countries covered in this study.

I Overview

In recent years, the issue of pension reform has been high on the agenda of many countries. To a large extent, this reflects common concerns regarding demographic trends of declining birthrates and increasing life expectancies that have shed serious doubt on the sustainability of current pension systems. Most countries have attempted to shore up their pay-as-you-go (PAYG) systems through some combination of reduced lifetime benefits and higher social taxes.

For some countries—including the Baltics—the search for solutions to the long-run problems facing pension funds has led to consideration of more fundamental reforms, in particular, a move toward the "three-pillar" pension system initially adopted by Chile in the early 1980s and promoted by the World Bank. Under such a scheme, the first pillar, aimed at providing a pension on a pay-as-you-go basis, is essentially a scaled-down version of the existing mandatory pension scheme. The second pillar aims to supplement this pension through a mandatory fully funded (defined contribution) plan, financed by a diversion of a portion of the payroll tax. The third pillar is designed to stimulate voluntary retirement savings, including through various tax advantages, and with public involvement limited to oversight and regulation.

A number of potential advantages have been ascribed to this type of pension scheme, including increased retirement income and national savings, and enhanced efficiency of capital and labor markets. However, a move to a fully funded scheme also imposes important costs, in particular on the current generation and the budget. The net effect on the welfare of present and future generations is therefore difficult to assess and in any case depends crucially on the specifics of the reform. The introduction of a mandatory fully funded (FF) scheme does not, however, in and of itself solve the problems associated with aging societies. Whether such a reform would be more effective in this regard than a policy aimed at shoring up the long-term finances of the PAYG system depends on several factors, including the extent to which the FF pension can increase national savings and output.

The Baltic countries have been in the forefront of transition economies in their pursuit of pension reform. They have taken important steps to shore up the long-run financial health of their existing pension funds and made preparations for the implementation of a three-pillar scheme. A review of their efforts to date provides an opportunity to assess possible benefits and pitfalls of pension reform, in particular for other transition economies. Further, as the Baltic countries are still in the process of reform and, in fact, have yet to make a number of crucial decisions regarding the ultimate design of their new pension systems, this is an opportune time to revisit the objectives of the reform and examine in detail the trade-offs among these goals that will inevitably be faced as the Baltics move forward.

Upon regaining their independence, the Baltics inherited the pension system of the Soviet Union. Section II examines this inherited pension scheme and initial attempts to reform its shortcomings, which included very low retirement age, complex benefit rules, and lax eligibility requirements. These flaws in pension design became dramatically apparent early in the transition as rapid inflation combined with a decline in economic activity limited the adequacy of pension benefits and brought into doubt the sustainability of the pension systems. While differing in important details, initial efforts to shore up the long-term finances of the Baltic pension systems have relied on reducing or slowing the growth of benefits, raising retirement ages or otherwise tightening eligibility for benefits, and establishing closer links between individual contributions and benefits in order to reduce labor market distortions and enhance collection of payroll taxes.

While the reforms did, to a significant degree, achieve the objective of putting the finances of the pension funds on a sounder footing, they have proved politically difficult to sustain. Ad hoc benefit increases, as well as continued difficulties in collecting payroll taxes, have tended to erode early gains. These difficulties, combined with the recognition that demographic trends in the Baltics are unfavorable, led to the view that more fundamental reforms would be required to ensure a sustainable pension system with adequate income for retirees.

In the mid-1990s, all three countries began to plan their eventual move to a three-pillar system. While all three countries have passed legislation to put in place voluntary private pension plans—the third pillar—and Latvia and Estonia are likely to implement their fully funded second pillar in 2001–2002, fundamental questions about the design of this fully funded scheme remain open. Section III outlines the progress made in the Baltics to date in this second stage of pension reform, examines the potential benefits and costs of this reform, and discusses the main considerations for each of a number of design decisions that will be made in the next several years.

The introduction of a fully funded pension scheme can have important macroeconomic effects. In Section IV, the potential implications for pension reform on savings and the savings-investment balance are analyzed, and it is shown that the impact depends very much on how that reform is financed. In particular, under the assumption that individuals are neither fully forward-looking nor completely myopic, a tax-financed move from a pay-as-you-go pension system toward a fully funded plan would tend to increase aggregate savings, while a debt-financed reform would reduce aggregate savings.

Given the potentially important macroeconomic impact of pension reforms, economic policy design should carefully consider their implications. Section IV argues that a pension reform should be evaluated in terms of whether it improves the long-run sustainability of the public finances, and so should be interpreted in the context of an intertemporal budget constraint, incorporating both the PAYG and FF schemes. At the same time, the financing of pension reform must also be consistent with prudent macroeconomic and debt management policy over the shorter term.

II Reform of the Pay-As-You-Go Pension Systems

PAYG in Early Transition Years

The Baltic states inherited a PAYG pension system from the Soviet Union (Box 2.1). Economic developments of the early 1990s had a tremendous impact on the pension systems in all transition economies, including the Baltic countries. Economic depression accompanied by growing unemployment (open and hidden) undercut the pension system's financing while adding large numbers of new beneficiaries.[1] At the same time, high inflation rates that were not immediately fully matched by nominal pension increases contributed to a sharp decline in the real value of pensions and flattening of benefits across different groups of beneficiaries.[2]

The pension systems were also hampered by problems of tax compliance. Decentralization of economic management and privatization of state enterprises undercut, at least initially, the state's ability to enforce tax collection, while low real wages, high unemployment, inflation, and uncertain political and economic prospects provided additional incentives to both employers and employees to avoid paying payroll taxes. In all three countries, pension system dependency ratios (that is, the number of pensioners divided by the total number of declared employed) were much higher than the demographic dependency ratio (the share of persons over 60 years divided by the number of people between 15 and 59 years), reflecting extensive early retirement and a sizable share of informal sector activity.[3] Partly as a result, the tax authorities managed to collect only about 70–75 percent of what theoretically could have been collected with full compliance.

In addition, the pension systems became, over time, the most important de facto (if not de jure) sources of welfare benefits to the growing number of unemployed and poor. To counter declining economic activity and rising unemployment, most transition economies, including the Baltics, relaxed or bent pension rules to provide benefits to displaced older workers (Table 2.2).[4] This use of the pension system to deal with rising unemployment arose from serious shortcomings in alternative social protection schemes,[5] including unemployment insurance, as well as the lack of financial and real assets owned by the unemployed and retired in the Baltics.[6]

Given these pressures, it is not surprising that pension spending was high and rising in the early years of transition. In Latvia, for example, pension spending rose by 4 percentage points of GDP over the period 1991–95, increasing to over 10 percent of GDP. In the two other Baltic countries, pension expenditures were more modest at 6–7 percent of GDP (Tables 2.3–2.5). This difference reflected both a somewhat worse demographic profile for Latvia and, by 1995, a higher average replacement rate (Tables 2.6–2.8). In all three

---

[1]The official rate of unemployment jumped from virtually zero in all Baltic countries in 1990 to about 10 percent in 1995 in Estonia, and 7 percent in Latvia and Lithuania. These official figures exclude those who were allowed to retire via disability, as well as the hidden unemployed who remained on their employers' payrolls.

[2]In Latvia, the average monthly pension rose 15.5 times between 1990 and 1992. In contrast, the average value of the CPI index rose 23.6 times during the same period. As a result, the real value of the average pension declined by 35 percent over this period.

[3]In Estonia, in 1995, for example, these ratios were, respectively, 57 percent and 37 percent.

[4]In Latvia, the number of pensioners rose from 610,000 in 1990 to 660,000 in early 1993, with over half of this increase attributed to a rise in disability pensioners. In Estonia, the number of pensioners increased from 360,000 in 1990 to 387,000 in 1993, with about 40 percent of the increase from higher disability rolls. It was also hoped that such early retirement would provide the scarce employment opportunities to younger entrants; the retirement age was either officially lowered or loopholes were permitted, and a large number of workers were made eligible to collect disability pensions.

[5]Until 1990, none of the centrally planned economies had faced large-scale open unemployment. The limited social protection schemes that did exist operated on the basis of state enterprises and were mostly focused on assisting families in distress.

[6]At end-1992, Latvian households held about 15 lats per person in bank deposits, equal to about 10 percent of the average annual pension. In 1998, about 80 percent of pensioners' income still came from social transfers. (Central Statistical Bureau of Latvia, 1998). In contrast, 1995 U.S. data on the wealth distribution indicate that households headed by 55 to 64 year olds had a median net worth of $110,000 compared with $11,400 for households headed by those under 35 (see Federal Reserve Board, 1997).

II REFORM OF THE PAY-AS-YOU-GO PENSION SYSTEMS

> **Box 2.1. The Pension Systems at Independence**
>
> Upon regaining independence, all three Baltic states inherited from the Soviet Union a standard, publicly managed, PAYG pension system. Under this system, administered by a state agency and financed by mandatory payroll taxes, those who worked paid for the benefits of current pensioners. Pensions were granted for several reasons; old-age, disability, and survivors' pensioners were the three largest groups of benefit recipients. The pension system provided multiple retirement and benefit rules; while the standard retirement age was set at 60 for men and 55 for women, employees of heavy industry and mining, teachers, police, and other categories of employees could retire earlier. The initial pension benefit was typically based on years of service and earnings during the most recent years preceding retirement. However, years of service and earnings were adjusted to account for service in difficult conditions, and years of service included credit for noncontributory periods, such as child care, university studies, or military service. Benefit rules favored certain occupational groups, and some sectors offered supplementary benefits to their former employees. These occupation-related supplements contributed to large differences in benefits among pensioners with similar education, work tenure, and preretirement incomes. In general, the system was perceived as redistributive, with notional rates of return much higher for workers with relatively low labor income and even negative for high wage earners. (This argument is often challenged as lower-educated wage earners start contributing social taxes much earlier in their careers and contribute for longer periods.)
>
> While pension benefits were relatively generous, it is important to note that pensioners in the Soviet Union and other central and eastern European (CEE) transition countries relied almost exclusively on the state pensions for income during retirement. Under the Soviet Union's economic system, individuals were not expected, or even allowed, to accumulate meaningful financial assets during working years (see Table 2.1). While households could save for purchases of major "big-ticket" items, such as appliances, cars, or, to a limited degree, housing, saving to derive capital income was not permitted.
>
> Until the late 1980s, the PAYG systems in the Soviet Union and most other CEE countries were financially stable, generating financial surpluses that were used to finance other parts of the government. High tax compliance was virtually assured because almost all employees worked for state-controlled institutions. Also, the relatively favorable demographic situation and high employment levels supported the financial stability of the system. In particular, in the three Baltic states, the elderly (55 years and older) comprised only 22.7 percent of the population in 1990 while, as a result of the baby boom during the 15 years following 1945, 41 percent of the population was of working age (between 25–54 years old).

countries, financial balance was largely maintained through a combination of high payroll taxes, relatively low replacement rates, and increased transfers from the central government. Looking forward, however, it was clear that demographic pressures would make it increasingly difficult to maintain this balance without substantial reforms.

Reforming the PAYG System

The stabilization of their economies in the mid-1990s allowed the Baltics to begin to focus on longer-term issues, in particular the sustainability of their existing pension systems. The large number of "baby boomers" born in the 1950s was expected to provide the PAYG system with significant financial surpluses during the first decade of the 21st century. If the existing parameters of the pension plan were left unchanged, however, the retirement of these baby boomers would lead to unsustainable deficits in the PAYG system.[7] The demographic situation in the Baltics was further complicated by a sharp drop in birthrates in the 1990s, with total fertility per woman declining from over 2 in the late 1980s to 1.2 in Latvia, 1.3 in Estonia, and 1.5 in Lithuania in 1999.[8] Finally, life expectancy at retirement is projected to continue increasing gradually, as the Baltic health systems modernize and the standard of living increases.[9] As a result, for the Baltic states as a whole, the share of the 25–54 year olds in total population is projected to first increase from 41.6 percent in 2000 to 43.1 percent in 2010 and then decline

---

[7] A PAYG system cannot technically go bankrupt. However, political claims for pension payments can far exceed actual revenues.

[8] The fertility rate in the Baltics is projected to increase to about 1.6 in 2010. The fertility rate in the neighboring Scandinavian countries stands at 1.7 in Finland and 1.8 in Sweden and was projected to decline to about 1.5 and 1.7, respectively, in 2010. The fertility rate is projected to remain under 1.7 for most of the central and eastern European countries through 2010.

[9] Life expectancy at birth is projected to increase by about 2–3 years in all transition economies over the next ten years. In Estonia life expectancy declined from 64.4 years for men and 74.8 years for women in 1991 to 61.1 for men and 73.1 for women in 1994 and recovered to 64.4 for men and 75.5 for women in 1998. Similarly, in Latvia and Lithuania, life expectancy for both men and women declined sharply in 1991–94, but has recovered and exceeds its 1991 levels.

Table 2.1. The Baltic States: Household Wealth Held in Bank Deposits

	1991	1992	1993	1994	1995	1996	1997	1998	1999
Bank deposits per person									
Estonia (krooni per person)	434.7	934.0	586.9	1,124.7	1,828.9	2,975.2	4,995.7	6,649.6	7,582.4
Latvia (lats per person)	...	...	...	87.6	94.4	46.8	63.6	89.5	96.5
Lithuania (litai per person)	...	...	152.7	369.7	604.2	546.4	700.0	861.9	1,178.7
Average bank deposits to monthly pension (percent)									
Estonia	...	533.7	169.6	235.8	256.9	308.9	454.2	537.6	501.5
Latvia	...	...	...	354.0	312.8	123.8	150.5	174.6	165.9
Lithuania	...	...	185.1	313.6	400.1	284.6	288.5	299.5	380.0
Memorandum items:									
Household deposits with bank									
Estonia (millions of krooni)	681	1,442	890	1,686	2,714	4,371	7,284	9,640	10,937
Demand	7	204	536	843	1,274	2,236	3,653	3,877	4,586
Time deposits	3	19	126	327	415	789	1,280	2,227	2,288
Savings deposits	273	104	39	63	82	84	223	531	461
Foreign currency[1]	397	1,116	189	453	943	1,262	2,128	3,005	3,601
Latvia (thousands of lats)	...	...	...	224,798	238,710	117,143	157,669	220,019	235,507
Demand	...	...	...	41,650	71,989	39,708	52,622	73,368	76,559
Foreign currency	...	...	...	115,307	92,293	23,008	27,684	36,218	38,788
Time deposits	...	...	...	67,841	74,428	54,427	77,362	110,433	120,160
Lithuania (millions of litai)	...	...	570	1,376	2,245	2,027	2,594	3,192	4,361
Demand	...	...	179	286	409	428	574	833	1,121
Foreign currency	...	...	332	592	1,266	1,121	1,449	1,703	2,294
Time deposits	...	...	59	498	569	477	571	656	946

Source: International Financial Statistics.
[1]Foreign currency deposits of the private sector.

to 38.5 percent in 2040 (Figures 2.1–2.4). During the same period, the share of the population 55 years and older will increase dramatically, from 25.3 percent in 2000 to 38.3 percent in 2040.

The push to reform the Baltic pension systems was given increased impetus by a number of other specific factors. First, while unemployment rates had begun to decline, a large number of potential workers lacked the incentive to give up early retirement or disability pensions as they could both work (often in the informal sector) and draw benefits. Second, since pensions depended only on years of service and not on the level of contributions, the pension systems provided little incentive for employees to contribute into the system or pressure their employers to comply with social tax rules.[10] Third, high payroll taxes not only discouraged tax compliance and encouraged the growth of the shadow economy but also tended to increase labor costs.[11] Fourth, the share of pension expenditure in total government outlays was relatively high, and changing fiscal priorities—in particular growing demand for infrastructure investment, education and medical services, and the need to finance preparations for EU accession—made the search for budgetary savings in the pension area unavoidable. Finally, the push to limit the relative size of pension expenditures was aided by a growing relative affluence of pensioners compared with other social groups, in particular families with young children.[12]

---

[10]In Latvia, between 1991 and 1995, the number of persons for whom contributions were being paid had declined by almost 50 percent. Further, many employers falsely reported that they paid minimum wages and paid contributions based on these wages.

[11]In 1996, social (payroll) tax rates in the Baltics varied from 31 percent of gross wages in Lithuania to 38 percent in Latvia. The pension component was 20 percent for Estonia and Latvia, and 23.5 percent for Lithuania. Within the Baltic countries, Russia and other countries of the former Soviet Union (BRO), the payroll tax was highest in Ukraine, at 52 percent (32.6 percent for pensions) and lowest in Lithuania and Turkmenistan, at 31 percent. In major industrialized countries (the U.S., Japan, Germany, France, Italy, the United Kingdom, and Canada) the payroll tax rates varied from 4.6 to 26.2 percent.

[12]In Latvia, for example, in 1996, the incidence of poverty in households headed by someone 65 or older was 37 percent compared with 40 percent for all households and 48 percent for households with a head 15–39 years old (see Gassmann, 2000).

II   REFORM OF THE PAY-AS-YOU-GO PENSION SYSTEMS

Table 2.2. The Baltic States: Impact of Economic Crisis on the Number of Pensioners

	1990	1991	1992	1993	1994	1995	1996	1997	1998	1999
	(Percent)									
Pensioners as percentage of employed[1]										
Estonia	44.6	48.8	54.1	55.9	57.4	58.0	57.8	58.5	61.0	63.6
Latvia	43.3	46.4	51.0	55.2	61.2	63.7	65.1	64.0	63.2	63.4
Lithuania	47.4	47.9	48.0	50.4	54.2	54.7	56.1	59.3	65.0	...
Ratio of disability pensioners to all pensioners										
Estonia	10.8	...	...	12.9	13.7	14.1	15.0	15.5	16.3	17.5
Latvia	11.0	13.4	15.5	15.7	15.7	15.5	14.9	14.2	13.7	13.4
Lithuania	13.0	12.7	13.9	14.3	14.7	15.5	15.8	15.4	14.8	...
	(Thousands)									
Memorandum items:										
Total number of pensioners (average)										
Estonia	361	374	383	387	376	375	375	374	375	378
of which: disability	39	...	...	50	52	53	56	58	61	64
Latvia	610	648	661	665	663	666	662	664	660	653
of which: disability	67	87	102	104	104	103	98	94	90	87
Lithuania	879	909	891	897	907	898	930	990	1,076	...
of which: disability	114	116	124	129	133	139	147	152	159	...
	(Annual percentage change)									
GDP growth rate										
Estonia	...	−11.8	−21.6	−8.2	−2.0	4.3	4.0	10.6	4.7	−1.4
Latvia	...	−10.4	−35.2	−14.9	0.6	−0.8	3.3	8.6	3.9	0.1
Lithuania	...	−5.7	−21.3	−16.2	−9.8	3.3	4.7	7.3	5.1	−3.3
	(Thousands)									
Number of registered unemployed (end of period)										
Estonia	...	0.9	14.9	16.2	15.6	15.2	18.5	19.3	18.8	28.2
Latvia	...	...	31.3	76.7	83.9	83.2	90.8	84.9	111.4	109.5
Lithuania	...	4.7	20.7	30.5	65.7	109.0	124.5	104.5	113.7	148.7
	(Percent)									
Unemployment rate (end of period)										
Estonia	0.6	1.5	3.7	6.7	7.6	9.8	10.1	9.8	9.6	11.9
Latvia	...	...	...	5.8	6.5	6.6	7.2	7.0	9.2	9.1
Lithuania	...	...	...	...	3.7	6.1	7.1	5.9	6.4	8.4

Source: National statistical agencies and staff estimates.
[1]Includes both full- and part-time employment.

Starting in the mid-1990s, all three Baltic countries began reforms primarily addressed at scaling down the PAYG system's expenditures and establishing a closer link between lifetime contributions and benefits. New formulas to link retirement benefits to past contributions were imposed, schedules for gradually raising the retirement age were put in place, indexation rules were modified to help ensure sustainability, and rules governing eligibility for benefits were gradually tightened. The most comprehensive, and earliest, reform was carried out in Latvia, while Estonia and Lithuania initially addressed pension reform in a more piecemeal fashion. However, at least some of the initial benefits of reform in Latvia were undone by subsequent ad hoc increases in pension benefits.

In each case, these reforms have been carried out within a broader framework envisaging the eventual introduction of a three-tier system. The first tier would be a modified PAYG system, with stronger links to contributions and a minimum pension to protect the lifetime poor. The second tier would be a fully funded system of privately managed savings accounts financed by a portion of the payroll tax. The third tier would be voluntary, privately managed pensions, organized primarily through employers (see Section III and Box 3.1).

Table 2.3. Estonia: Financial Performance of the Social Insurance Fund

	1993	1994	1995	1996	1997	1998	1999
	(Millions of krooni)						
Revenue and grants	2,084	3,017	3,900	4,801	5,723	6,781	7,041
Contributions	1,519	2,171	2,917	3,818	4,494	5,339	5,520
Grants from central government	517	683	769	910	1,031	1,403	1,505
Other[1]	49	162	214	73	198	38	15
Expenditure	1,961	2,611	3,714	4,941	5,744	6,563	7,790
Pensions	1,440	1,970	2,908	4,067	4,728	5,306	6,460
Old-age	1,211	1,619	2,389	3,322	3,860	4,303	5,285
Disability	158	219	340	467	556	664	863
Survivors	50	69	108	138	161	186	229
Other	21	63	71	140	151	153	83
Family benefits	479	586	769	865	1,007	1,159	1,146
Other	42	55	37	9	9	98	184
Balance	123	406	186	–140	–21	216	–749
	(Percent of GDP)						
Revenue and grants	9.6	10.2	9.6	9.2	8.9	9.2	9.3
Expenditure	9.1	8.8	9.1	9.4	8.9	9.0	10.3
Pensions	6.7	6.6	7.1	7.8	7.4	7.2	8.6
Family benefits	2.2	2.0	1.9	1.6	1.6	1.6	1.5
Balance	0.6	1.4	0.5	–0.3	0.0	0.3	–1.0
	(Percent of general government expenditure)						
Expenditure	22.4	21.6	21.9	23.3	23.9	22.5	23.9
Pensions	16.5	16.3	17.1	19.1	19.6	18.2	19.8
Family benefits	5.5	4.8	4.5	4.1	4.2	4.0	3.5
Memorandum items:							
Deposits of the SIF (in millions of krooni)[2]	...	...	...	772	751	967	...
General government expenditure and net lending (in millions of krooni)[3]	8,747	12,082	16,979	21,242	24,075	29,113	32,623
General government expenditure (in percent of GDP)	40.5	40.8	41.7	40.5	37.2	39.7	43.3
Nominal GDP	21,610	29,645	40,705	52,446	64,324	73,325	75,360

Sources: Social Insurance Fund and Ministry of Finance; and IMF staff estimates and projections.
[1]Largely interest income from Social Insurance Fund's bank deposits.
[2]End-year stock. In 1998, including EEK 180 million of deposits in closed banks.
[3]Includes net lending.

Strengthening the Link Between Contributions and Benefits

Each of the Baltic countries has moved to reduce the redistributive element of their pension systems by linking individual pension benefits to lifetime contributions. The introduction of such a link was aimed at improving tax compliance, including by providing incentives for participation in the formal labor market and enhancing the transparency of the pension system. Reforms in Latvia[13] made this link most pronounced, while the pensions systems in Estonia and Lithuania continued to include significant elements of redistribution.

In 1995, Latvia became the first CEE country to implement the reform of its PAYG pension system based on the introduction of the "notional defined contribution system".[14] The new PAYG system was designed to mimic a contribution-based pension that

---
[13]See Fox and Palmer (1999).

[14]Legislation for implementing the first tier was approved by parliament in November 1995 and took effect in January 1996.

II REFORM OF THE PAY-AS-YOU-GO PENSION SYSTEMS

Table 2.4. Latvia: Financial Performance of the Social Fund

	1993	1994	1995	1996	1997	1998	1999
	(Millions of lats)						
Revenue	168	236	291	328	381	427	453
Social tax	168	236	291	328	381	427	453
Expenditure	195	271	275	320	361	430	499.8
Pensions and family benefits	141	200	239	299	341	402	450
Pensions	141	200	239	299	341	402	450
Other	54	71	36	20	20	28	50
Balance	−27	−35	16	8	20	−4	−48
	(Percent of GDP)						
Revenue and grants	11.4	11.6	12.4	11.6	11.6	11.9	12.4
Social tax	11.4	11.6	12.4	11.6	11.6	11.9	12.4
Expenditure	13.3	13.3	11.7	11.3	11.0	12.0	13.6
Pensions	9.6	9.8	10.2	10.6	10.4	11.2	12.3
Balance	−1.9	−1.7	0.7	0.3	0.6	−0.1	−1.3
	(Percent of general government expenditure)						
Expenditure	37.1	34.7	28.9	29.0	27.1	27.7	29.0
Pensions	26.9	25.6	25.1	27.1	25.6	25.9	26.1
Memorandum items:							
General government expenditure and net lending (millions of lats)	525	780	952	1,104	1,332	1,553	1,724
General government expenditure (percent of GDP)	35.8	38.2	40.5	39.0	37.2	43.4	47.1
Nominal GDP (millions of lats)	1,467	2,042	2,349	2,829	3,275	3,580	3,662

Sources: Social Fund and Ministry of Finance; and IMF staff estimates and projections.

would be offered in the private sector by an efficient insurance company. The system provides individual accounts to all workers paying the social tax, with those contributions earmarked for the pension system credited to these accounts. In fact, however, social tax payments are used to pay benefits to current retirees, with the individual accounts serving as a record-keeping mechanism. The "capital" in each account earns a rate of return equal to the growth of the sum of wages on which contributions are collected (the contribution wage base), and participants receive annual statements of their contributions and accumulated "savings." At retirement, the pension paid is equal to the total capital in the person's account, divided by the projected life expectancy of the beneficiary on retirement.[15]

Some element of redistribution was maintained in Latvia through the introduction of a minimum guaranteed pension. All those who reach the age of 65 (and those who reach 60 and have 10 years of service) are eligible for this pension, with benefits set at the level of the social assistance pension. Since April 1, 1998, this pension has provided about 30 lats (US$50) per month.

Hidden subsidies in the form of pension credits for noncontributory periods were also removed. All such subsidies were made explicit, as contributions to the pension fund for time spent in higher education, in military service, or at home taking care of children, are made through transfers from the state budget, with contributions based on the minimum wage. The cost of these transfers to the state budget is estimated at roughly 0.3 percent of GDP per year.

---

[15]In the transition period, the PAYG pension scheme also includes pensioners receiving pensions granted under the previous legislation and financed from the funds generated by the current working population. Also, as a transition mechanism, retirement benefits of workers retiring in the years immediately following the reform were based only on contributions in the most recent 1–3 years.

Table 2.5. Lithuania: Financial Performance of the SoDra

	1993	1994	1995	1996	1997	1998	1999
	(Millions of litai)						
Revenue and grants	773	1,470	1,973	2,607	3,431	4,029	4,679
Revenue	773	1,470	1,973	2,607	3,431	4,029	4,423
Social tax	748	1,337	1,931	2,578	3,389	3,841	4,029
Grants from central government	...	...	...	...	...	...	256
Expenditure	785	1,453	1,972	2,644	3,461	4,061	4,478
Pensions and family benefits	669	1,230	1,642	2,157	2,812	3,419	3,711
Pensions	551	1,072	1,492	1,919	2,462	2,997	3,232
Family benefits	118	158	150	238	350	422	479
Other	116	223	330	488	649	642	767
Balance	−12	17	1	−37	−30	−32	201
	(Percent of GDP)						
Revenue and grants	6.7	8.7	8.2	8.3	8.9	9.4	11.0
Social tax	6.4	7.9	8.0	8.2	8.8	8.9	9.5
Expenditure	6.8	8.6	8.2	8.4	9.0	9.4	10.5
Pensions	4.7	6.3	6.2	6.1	6.4	7.0	7.6
Family benefits	1.0	0.9	0.6	0.8	0.9	1.0	1.1
Balance	−0.1	0.1	0.0	−0.1	−0.1	−0.1	0.5
	(Percent of general government expenditure)						
Expenditure	22.5	25.4	23.4	26.0	27.1	24.9	25.6
Pensions	15.8	18.8	17.7	18.9	19.2	18.4	18.5
Family benefits	3.4	2.8	1.8	2.3	2.7	2.6	2.7
Memorandum items:							
General government expenditure and net lending (millions of litai)	3,485	5,711	8,412	10,159	12,793	16,300	17,494
General government expenditure (percent of GDP)	35.4	37.4	36.8	34.2	33.7	39.4	40.7
Nominal GDP (million of litai)	11,590	16,904	24,103	31,569	38,340	42,990	42,597

Sources: Social Insurance Fund (SoDra) and Ministry of Finance; and IMF staff estimates and projections.

The Estonian authorities have also taken steps recently to link future pensions to contributions, albeit less closely than under the Latvian model. Beginning January 1, 1999, notional accounts were also introduced in Estonia. The new pension benefit formula consists of three components: a National Pension Rate (NPR) determined by parliament each fiscal year; a length of service component; and a contributions-related component, based on the worker's income subject to contribution relative to the average income subject to contributions.

The national pension is granted to individuals not eligible for old-age, work-incapacity, or survivors' pension, and provides minimum-income support for the elderly. Responsibility for these pensions has been shifted to the general budget, strengthening the insurance principles underlying the pension system. To qualify for the national pension, the person must reach retirement age and have resided in Estonia for at least 5 years prior to claiming the pension. The amount of the national pension is set as a percentage of the NPR and is determined by parliament every fiscal year; currently it is set at the equivalent of roughly US$47 per month.

The importance of length of service as well as the existence of a national pension rate in the benefit formula flatten the benefit structure and weaken the link between contributions and benefits in Estonia. It has been calculated, for instance, that even if the service-related component were completely phased out, an individual contributing 40 percent more than the average individual each year for 40 years would receive a pension only 13 percent higher in present value than that of the average person.

Under special circumstances, the government will make contributions to the pension fund at the rate

II REFORM OF THE PAY-AS-YOU-GO PENSION SYSTEMS

Table 2.6. Estonia: Pension Indicators

	1990	1991	1992	1993	1994	1995	1996	1997	1998	1999
Pensioners (thousands)	360.5	374.0	383.0	387.3	376.4	374.8	374.5	374.4	375.8	379.5
Working pensioners	102.4	...	94.6	69.5	56.4	54.6	53.1	55.5	...	...
Old-age pensioners	287.5	...	...	308.3	299.9	296.9	291.5	289.6	287.5	284.8
Disability pensioners	38.9	...	...	50.0	51.7	53.0	56.1	58.1	61.3	66.6
Survivors pensioners	17.2	...	...	20.7	18.0	20.1	21.5	21.8	22.4	23.2
Early retirement pensioners	...	...	...	5.9	5.0	3.2	3.2	2.7	2.7	3.2
Other	...	...	...	2.3	1.8	1.6	2.1	2.0	1.8	1.7
Disability pensioners/pensioners (percent)	...	...	...	12.9	13.7	14.1	15.0	15.5	16.3	17.5
System dependency ratio (pensioners/employed)	...	...	...	55.1	57.2	57.6	59.2	60.4	61.2	63.6
Average pension (krooni/month)	...	...	175.0	346.0	477.0	712.0	963.0	1,100.0	1,237.0	1,426.0
Average pension (change in percent)	...	...	...	97.7	37.9	49.3	35.3	14.2	12.5	15.3
Real average pension (change in percent)	...	...	...	8.7	–9.8	20.4	12.2	3.0	4.4	12.0
Real average pension index (1992=100)	...	...	100.0	108.7	98.0	118.0	132.3	136.3	142.3	159.3
Income replacement ratio[1]	...	...	31.9	32.5	27.5	30.0	32.3	30.8	30.0	35.2
Average pension (per month in US$)	...	...	14.0	26.2	36.7	61.9	80.3	79.3	88.0	97.0
Average pension (percent of subsistence minimum)	...	...	...	...	...	...	...	102.2	105.6	114.1
Memorandum items:										
Average net wage (krooni/month)	...	...	417.0	812.0	1,281.0	1,836.0	2,339.0	2,773.0	3,266.0	3,686.0
Average net wage (change in percent)	...	...	...	94.7	57.8	43.3	27.4	18.6	17.8	12.9
Real average net wage (change in percent)	...	...	...	5.7	10.1	14.4	4.3	7.4	9.7	9.6
Real average net wage index (1992=100)	...	...	100.0	105.7	116.4	133.1	138.9	149.1	163.5	179.1
Minimum wage (krooni)	...	...	300.0	300.0	450.0	450.0	680.0	845.0	1,100.0	1,137.5
Average net wage (US$/month)	...	...	33.0	62.0	99.0	160.0	195.0	200.0	231.0	274.0
Official per capita subsistence min. (krooni/month)	...	...	...	...	...	...	...	1,076.0	1,171.0	1,250.0
GDP (millions of krooni)	...	1.6	12.3	21.6	29.6	40.7	52.4	64.3	73.3	75.4
CPI (annual average)	...	...	1,069.0	89.0	47.7	28.9	23.1	11.2	8.1	3.3
Real GDP growth (percent)	...	...	–21.6	–9.0	–2.0	4.3	4.0	10.6	4.7	–1.4
Average exchange rate krooni/US$	...	...	12.5	13.2	13.0	11.5	12.0	13.9	14.1	14.7

Sources: Social Insurance Fund and Ministry of Finance; and IMF staff estimates.
[1]Average pension as a percentage of gross average wage.

applicable to the monthly minimum wage on behalf of qualifying individuals, including nonworking parents and the registered unemployed. Prior to the recent reforms these contributions awarded workers in these categories a full year of service and a significantly higher benefit. The new pension formula—which gives credit according to contributions paid—will correct this defect. The overall budget costs of the disability benefits, national pensions, and contributions for special categories of participants are estimated to be quite small.

In Lithuania, the reform effort also established a partial link between pension benefits and contributions. Under the 1994 reforms, pension benefits were calculated as a function of years of service (basic pension) and earnings (supplementary pension). This design was meant to ensure sufficient redistribution of benefits, while still introducing a relationship between lifetime earnings, contributions, and retirement benefits. Benefits were to be modest, providing at most a 40 percent replacement rate. While all citizens, including farmers, sole proprietors, and the self-employed, are covered by the basic pension, only persons employed under labor contracts are covered by the supplementary pension. To receive a full basic pension (set at 110 percent of minimum subsistence

Reforming the PAYG System

Table 2.7. Latvia: Pension Indicators

	1990	1991	1992	1993	1994	1995	1996	1997	1998	1999
Pensioners (thousands)	609.8	641.0	660.6	657.0	654.0	656.1	641.0	643.0	639.0	643.0
Working pensioners	...	...	...	...	...	48.5	55.4	61.2	66.9	70.2
Old-age pensioners	487.4	497.7	496.7	500.0	496.0	497.0	504.0	511.0	512.5	521.0
Disability pensioners	66.9	86.6	102.3	104.0	104.0	103.0	98.0	94.0	90.1	85.8
Survivors pensioners	38.7	32.0	28.0	26.0	29.0	30.0	30.0	29.0	29.0	28.5
Social	...	19.0	20.0	20.0	19.0	20.0	...	...	...	...
Service	1.2	5.0	7.9	7.2	6.5	6.1	6.1	6.3	5.1	5.2
Disability pensioners/pensioners (percent)	11.0	13.5	15.5	15.8	15.9	15.7	15.3	14.6	14.1	13.3
System dependency ratio (pensioners/employed)	0.4	0.5	0.5	0.6	0.6	0.6	0.7	0.6	0.6	0.6
Average pension (lats/month)	0.5	0.8	8.3	10.5	27.0	32.7	38.5	42.4	51.2	58.3
Average pension (change in percent)	...	62.5	964.1	26.5	157.1	21.1	17.7	10.1	20.8	13.9
Real average pension (change in percent)	...	−27.6	1.2	−39.5	89.2	−3.2	0.0	1.5	15.3	11.2
Real average pension index (1992=100)	136.4	98.8	100.0	60.5	114.5	110.8	110.9	112.5	129.8	144.2
Income replacement ratio[1]	29.8	76.7	38.6	22.2	37.6	36.5	39.0	35.3	38.4	41.3
Average pension (per month in US$)	...	...	11.3	15.6	48.2	62.0	69.8	73.0	86.9	99.6
Average pension (percent of subsistence minimum)	...	44.8	44.7	27.9	52.4	51.2	52.2	53.7	62.3	70.1
Memorandum items:										
Average net wage (lats/month)	...	2.8	24.2	41.0	60.3	73.4	78.7	88.3	97.5	102.7
Average net wage (change in percent)	...	...	764.3	69.5	47.1	21.7	7.2	12.3	10.4	5.4
Real average net wage (change in percent)	...	...	−17.8	−19.0	8.2	−2.7	−9.0	3.5	5.4	2.9
Real average net wage index (1992=100)	...	117.8	100.0	81.0	87.7	85.3	77.7	80.4	84.7	87.1
Minimum wage (lats/month)	...	1.1	8.2	15.0	22.0	28.0	35.5	38.0	42.0	50.0
Average net wage (US$/month)	...	...	32.9	60.9	107.8	139.3	142.7	152.0	165.3	175.5
Official per capita subsistence minimum (lats/month)	...	1.7	18.6	37.6	51.5	63.8	73.8	79.0	82.2	83.2
GDP (millions of lats)	...	0.1	1.0	1.5	2.0	2.3	2.8	3.3	3.6	3.7
CPI (annual average)	...	124.4	951.3	109.1	35.9	25.1	17.7	8.5	4.7	2.4
Real GDP growth (percent)	...	−10.4	−34.9	−14.9	0.6	−0.8	3.3	8.6	3.9	0.1
Average exchange rate lats/US$	...	...	0.7	0.7	0.6	0.5	0.6	0.6	0.6	0.6

Sources: Social Insurance Fund and Ministry of Finance; and IMF staff estimates.
[1] Average pension as a percentage of gross average wage.

level) workers had to have at least 30 years of service, with workers with 15 to 29 years of service receiving proportionally lower benefits, and those with less than 15 years not eligible for the basic pension.

The supplementary pension implicitly links benefits to contributions in Lithuania. Benefits depend on a worker's average lifetime earnings relative to average wage. Under this system, a record is kept of a worker's wages, expressed relative to the average national wage for each year of employment, with a maximum allowable multiple of average wage of 5. At retirement, a worker's 25 highest observations are averaged to compute the average lifetime earnings relative to the average wage. Benefits are computed by multiplying the worker's average lifetime relative earnings by the average wage in the period prior to retirement, with credit given at the rate of 0.5 percent for each year of service.

Raising the Retirement Age

In all three countries, gradual increases in retirement age play a key role in the strategy of ensuring

II REFORM OF THE PAY-AS-YOU-GO PENSION SYSTEMS

Table 2.8. Lithuania: Pension Indicators

	1990	1991	1992	1993	1994	1995	1996	1997	1998	1999
Pensioners (thousands)	879.0	909.2	890.8	896.8	907.3	898.4	930.1	989.7	1,076.3	1,041.6
Working pensioners										
Old-age pensioners	656.2	679.3	656.7	656.8	659.3	656.8	655.3	651.0	648.0	643.6
Disability pensioners	114.0	115.8	123.8	128.5	133.3	139.2	147.0	152.2	158.8	167.5
Survivors pensioners	59.4	56.0	48.4	48.0	52.6	49.7	47.8	44.1	40.7	...
Early retirement pensioners	...	...	...	...	...	...	...	...	...	...
Other	9.2	7.5	3.8	4.2	4.9	2.5	2.4	2.2	2.0	...
Disability pensioners/pensioners (percent)	13.0	12.7	13.9	14.3	14.7	15.5	15.8	15.4	14.8	16.1
System dependency ratio (pensioners/employed)	0.474	0.479	0.480	0.504	0.542	0.547	0.561	0.593	0.650	...
Average pension (litai/month)	1.09	6.65	29.42	82.50	117.90	151.00	192.00	242.60	287.80	310.16
Average pension (change in percent)	...	508.52	342.74	180.42	42.91	28.07	27.15	26.35	18.63	7.77
Real average pension (change in percent)	...	...	...	...	...	...	...	...	...	...
Real average pension index (1992=100)	...	...	...	...	...	...	...	...	...	...
Income replacement ratio[1]	36	97	57	50	36	31	31	31	31	31
Average pension (per month in US$)	...	10.72	17.39	19.28	29.60	37.75	48.00	60.65	71.95	77.54
Average pension (percent of subsistence minimum)	1.41	287.91	228.65	278.25	235.42	218.21	211.45	218.95	233.41	248.13
Memorandum items:										
Average net wage (litai/month)	...	7.6	57.5	183.3	364.6	516.0	688.8	851.9	1,022.4	1,074.8
Average net wage (change in percent)	...	...	656.6	218.8	98.9	41.5	33.5	23.7	20.0	5.1
Real average net wage (change in percent)	...	...	...	...	...	...	...	...	...	...
Real average net wage index (1992=100)	...	...	...	...	...	...	...	...	...	...
Minimum wage (litai/month)	...	5	17.0	32.7	56.5	134.6	240.0	374.2	417.5	430
Average net wage (US$/month)	...	12.4	34.0	42.8	91.5	129.0	172.2	213.0	255.6	268.7
Official per capita subsistence minimum (litai/month)	77.5	2.308	13	30	50	69	91	111	123	125
GDP (billions of litai)	0.5	0.4	3.4	11.6	16.9	24.1	31.6	38.3	43.0	42.6
CPI (annual average)	...	...	1,020.5	410.4	72.1	39.5	24.7	8.8	5.1	0.8
Real GDP growth (percent)	...	−5.7	−21.3	−16.2	−9.8	3.3	4.7	7.3	5.1	4.9
Average exchange rate litai/US$	...	0.6	1.7	4.3	4.0	4.0	4.0	4.0	4.0	4.0

Sources: Social Insurance Fund and Ministry of Finance; and IMF staff estimates.
[1]Average pension as a percentage of gross average wage.

long-term sustainability of the PAYG pension system. Changes were as follows:

- In Latvia, the 1995 pension legislation foresaw a gradual increase in retirement age for women from 55 to 60—the retirement age for men—by 2004, and it was anticipated that the retirement age would, in the longer term, increase to the age of 65 for both sexes. (Retirement age has subsequently been increased more rapidly. See Box 2.2.) In any case, as pension benefits were to be actuarially fair, so that expected lifetime benefits were unaffected by an individual's retirement age, the system provided incentives to work beyond these ages.[16] In addition, special early retirement rights for particular occupations were phased out.[17] The

---

[16]For example, assuming a constant wage, annual pension benefits would double when an individual worked until age 70 instead of 60.

[17]To compensate for this, the notional pension capital of eligible workers was increased to reflect their pre-reform early retirement right and years of service in the occupation. For example, for a man with 20 years of service in an occupation which pro-

Reforming the PAYG System

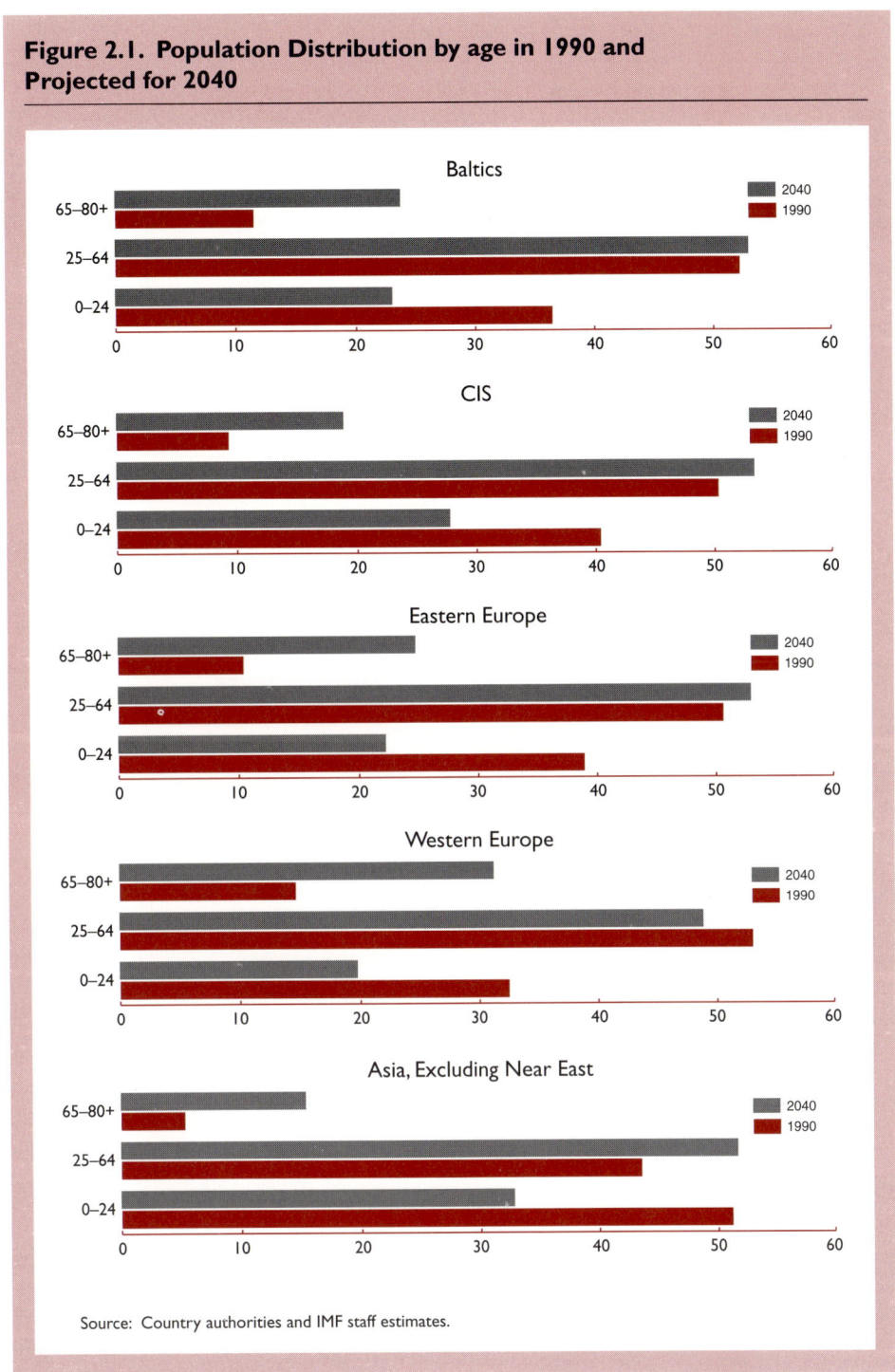

Figure 2.1. Population Distribution by age in 1990 and Projected for 2040

Source: Country authorities and IMF staff estimates.

minimum pension guarantee did not apply to anyone taking a pension before age 60. Those retiring early were entitled only to an actuarially fair pension; it was expected that most would find this pension to be so low that they would continue to work, greatly reducing the number of early retirees.

- In Estonia, starting on January 1, 1994, the normal retirement ages for men (60 years) and women (55

---

vided the right to retire at 50, the pension capital for those years would be increased by 20 percent (60/50).

II REFORM OF THE PAY-AS-YOU-GO PENSION SYSTEMS

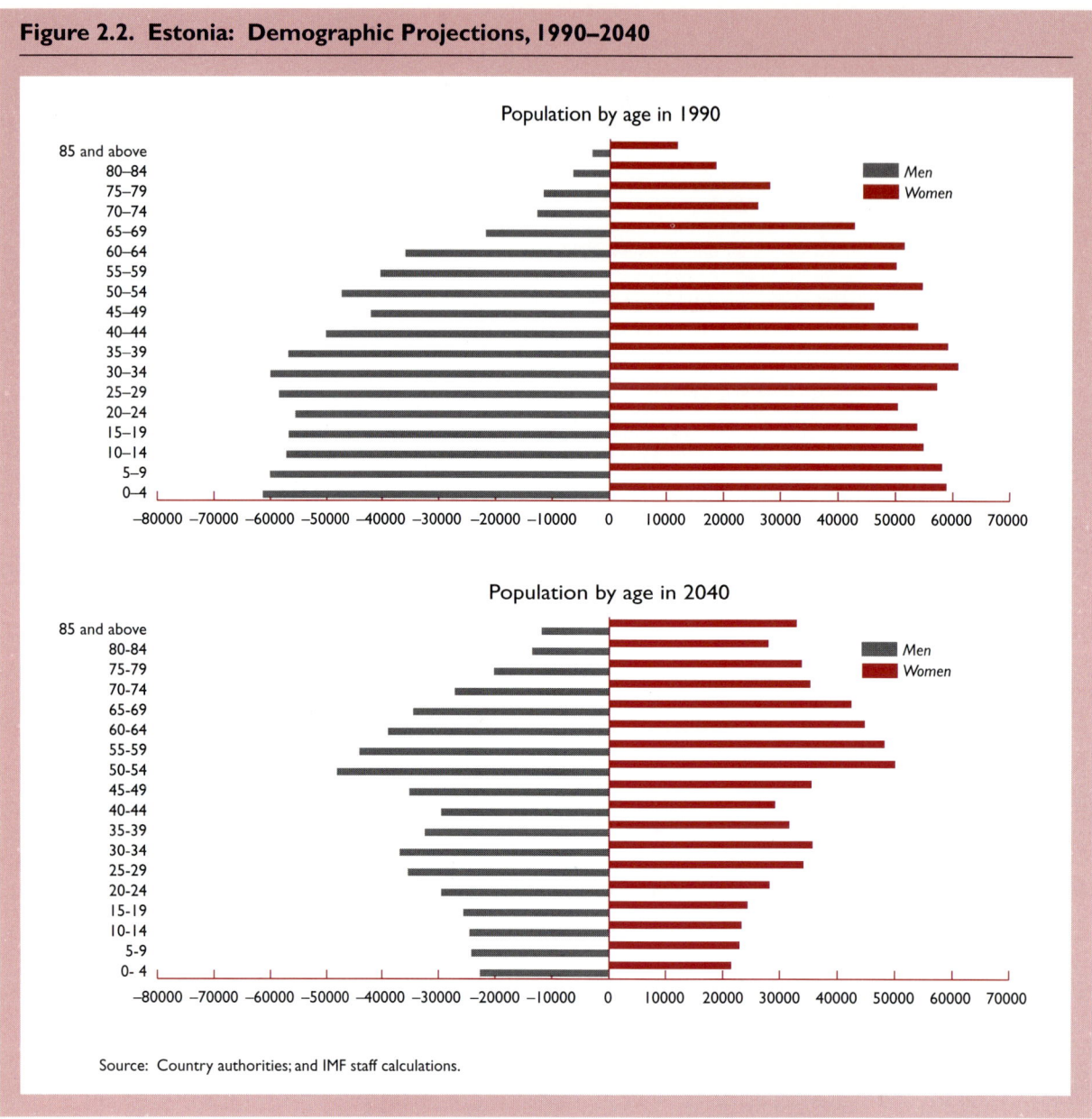

Figure 2.2. Estonia: Demographic Projections, 1990–2040

Source: Country authorities; and IMF staff calculations.

years) were revised each year by three months for men and six months for women, so that a retirement age of 63 years would be reached for men in 2006 and for women in 2010. The New Social Tax Act introduced the possibility of early retirement; an individual can retire up to three years before the statutory retirement age with a reduced pension. The adjustment factor is 0.4 percent per month in advance of normal retirement age, which is meant to be actuarially fair on average.

- In Lithuania, legislation was passed in 1994 to raise the retirement age from 55 to 60 at the rate of four months annually for women and from 60 to 62.5 at the rate of two months annually for men, with the ultimate retirement age attained by the year 2009. Subsequently, under a World Bank–supported Structural Adjustment Loan (SAL) program the government accelerated these increases at the rate of six months yearly for both men and women, and increased the retirement age for women further, to 62.[18] It was expected that the retirement age would have to increase to 65 by

---
[18]See World Bank (1998).

Figure 2.3. Latvia: Demographic Projections, 1990–2040

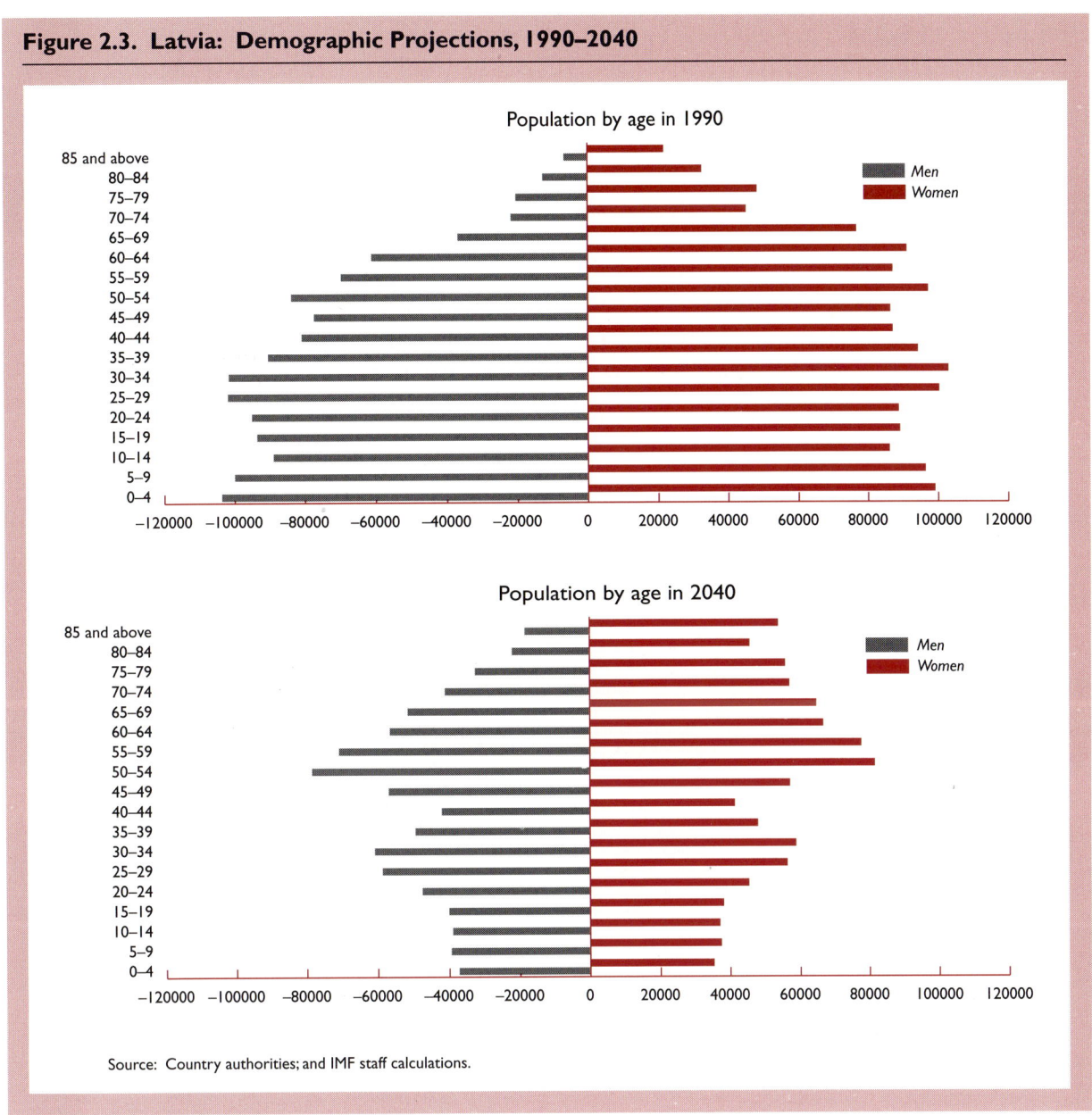

Source: Country authorities; and IMF staff calculations.

the year 2024 for men and women to ensure financial stability of the PAYG system.

Indexation Provisions

In the Baltics, where wages are low relative to industrial countries, but are expected to grow rapidly, an important issue is the extent to which retirees will share in productivity gains. To reduce the first pillar deficit, and allow an increase in the size of the second pillar over time, a government may wish to adopt at the outset a pension indexation formula that is below that of the wage growth rate. While such an indexing mechanism would have important benefits for the financial health of the PAYG scheme, it would imply a steady decline in the replacement rate for retirees relative to prevailing wage rates, although the replacement rate relative to the retirees' last wage could continue to grow in real terms, assuming that real wages grow economy-wide. If pension coverage falls too much relative to prevailing wages, such indexation schemes could generate political pressure for additional ad hoc benefit increases.

II REFORM OF THE PAY-AS-YOU-GO PENSION SYSTEMS

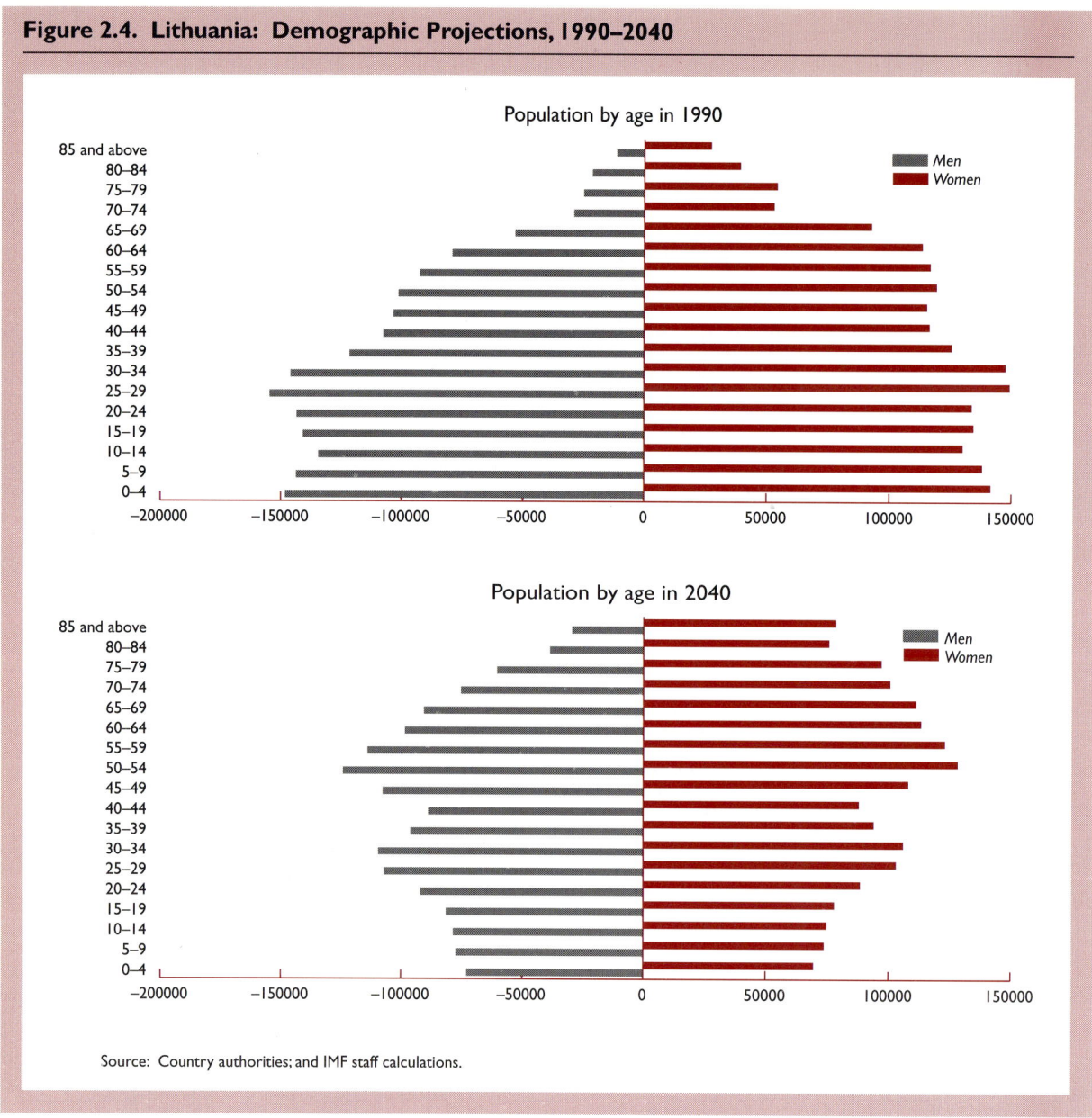

Figure 2.4. Lithuania: Demographic Projections, 1990–2040

Source: Country authorities; and IMF staff calculations.

In Latvia, affordability of the PAYG was reinforced through changes in its indexing provisions. During the accumulation period, contributions in the "notional" account are indexed to the inflow of resources to the pension system, so that liabilities do not grow more rapidly than revenues. Upon retirement, pensions are indexed to the Consumer Price Index (CPI) until 2002, and after that to a mix of wages and prices. This will improve the finances of the Pension Fund, and avoid rising liabilities during an economic downturn, but implies a declining replacement rate, relative to the prevailing wage, over time. Pensions are also adjusted for life expectancy, automatically adjusting to demographic changes.

Estonia has not yet developed a schedule for indexing pensions for inflation. Instead, pensions have been increased periodically, often before elections; there has been a political understanding that pensions would be maintained at about 40 percent of the average wage. The lack of explicit procedures is a serious potential weakness in the pension system, which is expected to be addressed under new legislation in 2000. Three possibilities are being considered: indexation to CPI, to the growth rate of

> **Box 2.2. Latvia: The 1999 Pension Amendments**
>
> In Latvia, problems with the transition rules following the 1995 pension reform contributed to higher-than-expected pension spending. In particular, the fact that pension capital for new retirees was based only on the most recent year or two of contributions provided a strong incentive for working pensioners to have their benefits recalculated based on most recent earnings while some employees near retirement age even borrowed money to make large contributions. In these ways, a few gained entitlement to pensions up to six times the average. Parliament responded by imposing a ceiling on all pension benefits of about three times the average wage. In addition, amendments introduced in 1999 prohibited pension recalculations, although this was not made retroactive.
>
> Several other changes were introduced, restoring some of the redistribution of the previous system, and chipping away at the sustainability that had been built into the pension reform. In particular, those who had contributed during the first years after the transition would have their capital valued at least at the average wage, even if their own wage was lower; and 80 percent of the guaranteed minimum pension was extended to all women retiring before age 60, regardless of the pension they should have received based on the benefit formula. The latter contributed to a more rapid-than-expected increase in the number of retirees in Latvia, and the provision is currently under review.
>
> The fall in tax revenues associated with the Russia crisis forced the Latvian government to reconsider the level of pension spending and develop proposals to restore the original intent of the reform—bringing the pension system into balance. In August 1999, the Latvia parliament passed a series of amendments to the pension law. The retirement age for men was to be gradually raised from 60 to 62 by January 1, 2002; and for women from 57.5 to 59 on January 1, 2000, and by 6 months each year until it reached 62 in 2006. The amendment cancelled the right to retire early (at age 55) available to women, and all working pensioners with monthly pensions above 60 lats were to lose benefits during 2000–05. The amendments also limited the eligibility for the minimum pension to those who contribute for more than 30 years. Other proposals included limiting cost-of-living indexation to once per year and returning to backward-looking indexation, and annulling special pension increases to pensioners who reached the age of 80.
>
> These amendments met with strong resistance from a number of opposition parties that forced a national referendum on the bill. In response, the government submitted to parliament and won approval for a softer package of amendments. Specifically, the speed at which the retirement age was to reach 62 for both men and women was reduced. Starting January 1, 2000, men could retire at 60.5 and starting July 1, the retirement age for women will increase to 58. The retirement age for both men and women will increase by six months annually until it reaches 62. At the same time, the revised amendments allowed men and women with at least 30 years of service to retire at the age of 60 (men) or two years before the official retirement age (women) at 80 percent of the full pension. The revisions also scaled down the penalty to working pensioners; such pensioners with monthly pensions above 60 lats will receive 60 lats rather than zero. The revisions also returned to the original policy of guaranteeing a minimum pension of 30 lats to all pensioners, but left unchanged the original proposals regarding indexation provisions and the elimination of increases to those over 80. While the final amendments were weaker than those originally proposed, they appear to have had a positive impact on the finances of the Pension Fund thus far in 2000.

the wage fund, or to a weighted average of the two. The last proposal has considerable merit in that it would reduce the liabilities to current pensioners with respect to full indexation to the wage fund but would still allow pensioners to partly benefit from the expected increases in real wages.

In Lithuania, pensions are indexed to a weighted average of two components. The first component is the minimum living level which is adjusted by the government on an ad hoc basis. The second component is based on the average wage in the economy.

Tightened Eligibility for Disability Pensions

In response to the rapid growth in the number of disability pensioners, the Baltic countries also moved to tighten eligibility for such pensions. In Estonia, modifications to the disability benefits were implemented in 1999, linking the work-incapacity pension to the length of service and the establishment of a minimum contribution period. Prior to this change, invalidity pensions were flat rate benefits determined by the degree of invalidity. The work-incapacity pension will be paid only to permanently work-incapable individuals, and will be paid only during the working age years. When the individual reaches the retirement age, the benefits will be switched to an old-age pension.[19]

---

[19]In parallel with these modifications, parliament approved the Social Benefits for the Disabled Act, which entered into effect on January 1, 2000, and establishes benefits for disabled individuals not qualifying for the work-incapacity pension.

II REFORM OF THE PAY-AS-YOU-GO PENSION SYSTEMS

Experience with Reforms to Date

The experience with pension reform in the Baltics has been mixed. On the one hand, increases in retirement age and tightening of eligibility for benefits strengthened the finances of the pension funds in all three countries. In Latvia, in particular, social fund deficits of nearly 2 percent of GDP in 1993–94 were converted to surpluses averaging about ½ percent of GDP during 1995–97 (Table 2.4). On the other hand, pension expenditures as a share of GDP were significantly higher in all three countries in 1999 than in 1995. Some reforms, in particular in Estonia, are still quite new, and their full effects have yet to be felt.

Gains from reform have also been partially undone by ad hoc benefit increases in Latvia and Estonia. In Latvia, with an election looming in the fall of 1998, the government used a portion of the fiscal surplus to increase pension indexation beyond that provided for in the law,[20] and pensioners received, in addition, a one-time increase averaging 15 percent. As a result, the social fund was in deficit in 1998–99, reserves were fully run down, and the pension fund had to borrow from the central government (Box 2.2). In Estonia, in late 1998, the parliament facing elections in early 1999 voted to increase average pensions by over 20 percent in real terms in 1999, contributing together with a recession to a deficit in the social fund of about 1 percent of GDP. These experiences underline the need for a rules-based approach to increases in pension benefits.

In Lithuania, the authorities have let benefits increase according to their formula. While several ad hoc adjustments to the minimum subsistence level (to which the basic pension is linked) led to a significant rise in pension spending, financial balance was generally maintained through economic growth. However, since the formula does not allow for a fall in pensions, with the fall in wages after the Russian crisis, the social insurance fund has more recently incurred deficits.

Taken together, while reform of the PAYG pillar has moved in the right direction, more needs to be done. Retirement ages should be increased further, and eventually reach industrial country levels. Benefit indexation should be set with due regard to its impact on PAYG finances and be taken out of the political arena. Finally, further strengthening of the link between contributions and benefits may lead to enhanced labor market efficiency and greater tax compliance.

---

[20]In addition, in November 1997, the government changed from adjusting for past CPI increases (backward indexation) to a combination of backward and forward-looking indexation. As a result, pensioners were given a one-time double indexation, totaling 7 percent. Further, in March 1998, the government announced an additional ad hoc indexation.

III Introduction of a Three-Pillar Pension System

While the early reforms of the Baltic PAYG systems were oriented at preserving the financial solvency of these systems, demographic trends led policymakers in the Baltics, as elsewhere, to look for alternatives to their pensions systems. A PAYG system remains solvent as long as the working generation is able and willing to share sufficient income with the retired generation. However, given expected population trends, it was viewed as unrealistic to expect future working generations, dwindling in absolute numbers, to continue to support an ever larger population of retirees to the same extent as at present. To ensure sustainability via a PAYG system would require further increases in the already high payroll tax rates—which would overburden the working generation, complicate social tax collection, and have an increasingly negative impact on work incentives[21]—or reductions in lifetime retirement benefits. As indicated in Table 3.1, maintaining a 40 percent replacement rate and a retirement age of 60 in the Baltics would eventually require that a payroll tax collect about 40 percent of gross wages, which would imply a tax rate well in excess of 40 percent.

Motivated in large part by the desire to address the demographic problems, all three Baltic states currently plan to move toward a three-pillar pension system in the future, along the lines recommended by the World Bank (see Box 3.1). This involves, first, a continued focus on a strengthening of the finances of the PAYG system and, second, the introduction of a fully funded pillar, which will become an important vehicle for retirement saving, especially for the currently young workers.

Introduction of a Three-Pillar System: Pros and Cons

Proponents of a move to a three-pillar system claim a number of potential gains from the introduction of a fully funded scheme. Such a plan is expected, inter alia, to provide higher levels of retirement income, enhance the efficiency of the economy, and increase transparency of the pension system.

Higher average returns on savings for retirement. It was anticipated that the move to an FF pension would help address the demographic challenges, as an FF system was expected to provide a higher rate of return than a PAYG plan. The rate of return on the FF system would, in the long run, depend on the economy-wide interest rate, or marginal productivity of capital, and—assuming that the pension scheme allows investment abroad—foreign interest rates. The implicit return in the PAYG system, on the other hand, depends on the growth of the labor force and average wages. Given the projected demographic trends, the former was expected to be significantly larger.[22]

It should be noted though, that over the long run the rate of return on capital also depends, in part, on demographic trends, so that simply moving to a fully funded scheme does not allow a country to "escape" demographics (Box 3.2).[23] A fully funded system may, however, be able to better handle the adverse domestic demographic trends of a country, provided that the mandatory private pension funds are allowed to invest internationally, and that the world's

---

[21]The size of the distortions introduced by the payroll tax would be expected to rise more than linearly with increases in the tax rate.

[22]It is argued that, in a dynamically stable economy, the return on capital (or real interest rate (r)) is generally higher than the real growth rate of the economy (g). If the opposite were true (that is, if $g > r$) those assets whose dividends grow with the economy would attain an infinite price, offering an arbitrage opportunity to private investors. Issues of private and public debt will eventually push the market yield r above g (see, for example, Hemming (1998)). Empirical evidence suggests that this is the case.

[23]In a closed economy, the pension burden of a future generation of workers is determined by the pensions that have to be paid and not by the way in which they are financed. When pensioners are making too large a claim on an economy's output, the working generation will likely scale down the pension contributions required to meet pension claims under the PAYG system. The result is not likely to be significantly different under a funded scheme, as the value of the assets held by pensioners in this case will fall as increasing numbers of pensioners attempt to sell assets to relatively fewer workers. See Brooks (2000).

III INTRODUCTION OF A THREE-PILLAR PENSION SYSTEM

Table 3.1. The Baltic States: Demographic Projections and Theoretical Burden of the Pay-As-You-Go Pension System

	Estonia				Latvia				Lithuania			
	1990	1999	2020	2040	1990	1999	2020	2040	1990	1999	2020	2040
	(Percent of gross wage and salary needed to support the pensioner population)											
Retirement at 60												
PAYG burden if pensions replace 25 percent working income[1]	12.7	16.3	19.9	25.6	13.0	15.7	19.2	25.0	11.8	13.4	16.6	23.5
PAYG burden if pensions replace 40 percent working income	20.3	26.1	31.8	40.9	20.8	25.1	30.7	40.0	18.8	21.4	26.6	37.7
PAYG burden if pensions replace 60 percent working income	30.4	39.1	47.7	61.4	31.2	37.6	46.0	60.0	28.2	32.1	39.9	56.5
Retirement at 65												
PAYG burden if pensions replace 25 percent working income	7.8	10.6	13.3	17.4	8.1	10.1	12.7	17.4	7.4	8.9	10.8	16.5
PAYG burden if pensions replace 40 percent working income	12.6	17.0	21.3	27.8	12.9	16.2	20.3	27.9	11.8	14.3	17.3	26.4
PAYG burden if pensions replace 60 percent working income	18.8	25.5	31.9	41.8	19.4	24.2	30.4	41.9	17.6	21.4	25.9	39.6
	(Percent)											
Population ratios												
Population over 60 to working-age population	28.4	33.4	41.3	57.3	29.1	35.1	42.9	56.0	26.4	30.0	37.2	52.7
Population over 65 to working-age population	17.6	21.8	27.7	39.0	18.1	22.6	28.4	39.1	16.5	20.0	24.2	37.0
Memorandum items												
Under age 15	22.3	17.7	15.9	12.2	21.5	17.3	16.3	12.5	22.6	19.4	17.7	13.7
Population 15–19	7.0	7.5	5.1	4.4	6.8	7.6	4.9	4.3	7.4	7.5	5.6	4.9
Population 16–59	60.6	61.7	59.5	55.8	60.8	61.2	58.6	56.1	61.3	62.0	60.0	56.5
Population 16–64	66.1	67.6	65.9	63.2	66.5	67.4	65.2	62.9	66.5	67.1	66.3	63.0
Over age 60	17.2	20.6	24.6	32.0	17.7	21.5	25.1	31.4	16.2	18.6	22.3	29.8
Over age 65	11.6	14.7	18.2	24.6	12.0	15.3	18.5	24.6	11.0	13.4	16.0	23.3
Working as a percentage of working-age population[2]	70.0	64.0	65.0	70.0	70.0	70.0	70.0	70.0	70.0	70.0	70.0	70.0
Contributing as a percentage of working[2]	80.0	80.0	80.0	80.0	80.0	80.0	80.0	80.0	80.0	80.0	80.0	80.0

Source: U.S. Census Bureau, International Data Base; and IMF staff projections.
[1] Gross wage and salary income, inclusive of social tax.
[2] Assumed.

demographic trends are more favorable than those of the home country.

Increased national savings rates. A switch to the FF pillar could stimulate savings above their current levels, raising output and potentially contributing in a solution to the demographic problem. Assuming that the government finances the ensuing first pillar deficit primarily through increased taxes or reduced expenditures, rather than via increased borrowing, private savings outside the second pillar might decline somewhat, but the net effect is expected to be a rise in national savings in both the short and long term (see Section IV). Nevertheless, the impact of these higher savings on domestic output may be marginal in small open economies such as the Baltics with ready access to international capital markets and large capital inflows.

Capital market development. It has been claimed that the rising investment needs of pension funds, together with the competitive setup of the privately managed funds, would eventually lead to deeper, more liquid and more competitive national capital markets. However, in the context of small open economies, such as the Baltics, it is questionable whether relying on domestic capital markets is necessary, or even an appropriate use of resources.[24]

---
[24] See Kotlikoff (1999)

Introduction of a Three-Pillar Pension System: Pros and Cons

> **Box 3.1. The World Bank Pension Model**
>
> All three Baltic countries have decided to adopt a three-pillar pension system to replace the PAYG systems that they inherited from the Soviet era. The three-pillar system has been actively promoted by the World Bank (1994), following the model adopted by Chile in the early 1980s. According to the Bank, the three-pillar system facilitates a separation of the income transfer function from the redistribution function of pension schemes, with each pillar having a different objective, as follows:
>
> - The first pillar is intended to provide a safety net for the elderly. It would be a mandatory, publicly run PAYG system (defined benefit), financed through social security contributions on wages. Benefits under this pillar may be universal or means tested, with the Bank having a preference for the latter;
> - The second pillar is to supplement first-pillar pension benefits through a fully funded system (defined contribution). It will also be financed through mandatory contributions on wages. The Bank favors privately run second-pillar schemes on the grounds that governments are likely to interfere in the investment decisions of pension funds for political ends rather than based on economic efficiency, thus using inefficiently "captive" resources.
> - The third pillar is designed to comprise private retirement savings options, with public involvement limited to regulation to ensure investor protection.
>
> Few governments in Eastern Europe have as yet tackled this entire agenda.[1] All of the Baltic countries, Albania, Georgia, and the Czech Republic have implemented some parts of it, but only Georgia, Kazakhstan, Hungary, Latvia, and Poland have to date adopted relatively complete pension reforms.
>
> ———
> [1]National Research Council, 1998.

> **Box 3.2. Intergenerational Transfers: Who Pays for the Pensions?**
>
> Over the long run, pensions must be paid out of national income, that is, domestic output and net factor income from abroad.
>
> - Under a PAYG system, the working generation pays for the retired generation's pension out of current income through the payroll tax.
> - Under an FF system, the working generation still pays for the retired generation's pensions, through interest and savings. First, the working generation pays interest on the economy's capital stock owned by the retirees (factor income). Second, the working generation buys the retired generation's share of the economy's capital stock. This is the workers' savings that form the basis of their pension benefits. In addition, the retired generation may receive pension income from abroad, if parts of their savings had been invested abroad.
> - The introduction of an FF system can provide a higher level of consumption to the working generation and a higher pension level to the retired generation if, and only if, the FF savings have a positive effect on economic growth. First, this positive effect can result from capital accumulation. Second, this positive effect can result from efficiency gains attributed to the FF system compared with the PAYG system.
> - A debt-financed move from a PAYG system to an FF system is unlikely to provide both a higher level of consumption to the working generation and a higher pension level to the retired generation. Since the FF savings are offset by the PAYG deficit, there is no growth effect resulting from capital accumulation. Any growth effect can only result from efficiency gains.

The expected accession of the Baltic countries to the European Union and the European Central Bank (ECB) over the next five or so years serves to underline this point.

Closer links between contributions and benefits reduce labor market distortions. It has been argued that, under an FF system, contributions may be viewed not as taxes, but rather as individual savings, so that labor market efficiency will increase in at least two ways. First, with retirement benefits dependent on lifetime contributions, the shift to an FF system might be expected to contribute to a shift of labor from the informal to the formal sector.[25] Second, as taxes are reduced, the overall supply of labor should also increase and the efficiency of the mix of productive inputs improve. However, this positive effect may not fully materialize. The second pillar is made mandatory because it is believed that individuals would otherwise undersave; at least some portion of the FF contribution may therefore be viewed as a tax, distorting optimal (short-run) behavior. The Chilean experience (Box 3.3) is consistent with this view.

———
[25]This effect could also be achieved under a PAYG system by introducing notional accounts which provide a link between contributions and pension benefits.

III INTRODUCTION OF A THREE-PILLAR PENSION SYSTEM

> **Box 3.3. Have Fully Funded Pension System Reforms Lived Up to Expectations?**
>
> FF systems have only been introduced relatively recently, and the evidence so far regarding their potential advantages over PAYG systems is mixed. Only in Chile has the FF scheme been in operation for a relatively long period of time (1981), whereas the other countries that have embarked on FF pension reforms have done so in the 1990s (for example., Colombia in 1993, Argentina in 1994, Peru in 1995, Uruguay in 1996, and Mexico in 1997).
>
> As regards the Chilean experience, there was, on the one hand, a marked development of Chile's capital market following the adoption of the FF scheme, boosting investments and GDP growth. The return on FF investments has also been relatively high, although it has moderated recently following a slowdown of the economy. On the other hand, contrary to expectations there has been no significant shift of labor from informal to formal markets, suggesting that social security contributions are only one among many disincentives for formal employment. Also, the empirical evidence in support of increased national savings following the introduction of fully funded systems is still lacking. In Chile, although private savings increased sharply in the late 1980s and early 1990s, a period that corresponds with the pension system reform, this was largely due to increased savings from firms, while households savings remained broadly flat.

Greater transparency and reduced political risks. The traditional PAYG system—as a defined benefit plan—is relatively inflexible in that it can be politically and legally quite difficult to reduce pension levels as the tax base declines and the fiscal burden increases. For example, as noted above, the Latvian government's attempt to cover the shortfall in the pension fund in mid-1999 by cutting eligibility for benefits led to a political crisis, which ultimately forced the government to scale back its plans. An FF pension system, however, allows benefits to adjust automatically when rates of return on accumulated assets change, taking the potential conflict between generations out of the political arena. However, it is possible that lower than expected returns on an FF pension scheme would generate political demands for action to increase retirement income through the budget.

Critics have raised a number of concerns related to FF schemes, focused largely on the transition costs of a move from a PAYG to an FF system. In addition, critics have placed doubt on the claims regarding increased economy-wide efficiency put forth by advocates of the three-pillar system. Rather than favoring an FF pension, PAYG proponents offer a number of recommendations to preserve the current systems, including raising retirement ages and reducing some benefits to bring the system's parameters up-to-date with rising life expectancy. Others have presented alternatives to the pension reform, which differ in at least some aspects from the World Bank's three-pillar model (see Box 3.4). Those who favor keeping the present system broadly unchanged argue that, in any case, an FF scheme is already available to anybody who wants to save voluntarily and appropriate tax legislation should be used to stimulate savings in the voluntary FF pillar. Among their specific criticisms of the three-pillar system are the following:

The move to a fully funded scheme would come at a significant cost for transition generations. While some portion of payroll tax revenue would be shifted to the FF pillar, current retirees (and older workers retiring under the old pension) would still need to have their benefits paid by current workers. In essence, the current working generation would be required both to support the current retirees and prefund a large part of its own retirement. This transition cost results from the fact that the first generation under a PAYG system receives a pension without having to contribute. The "last" generation—that is, the transition generation—has to pay for the first generation's pension and for its own pension as the "chain-letter" is broken. Given that the present working generation in the Baltics has already carried the burden of adjustment to a market-based economy, one could argue that this generation should not be additionally burdened with a pension reform. Nevertheless, the demographic picture suggests that there is currently a window of opportunity that would allow these transition costs to be shared by a large working-age cohort.

The efficiency gains of a pension reform replacing the PAYG with an FF system are ambiguous. For example, while the reform may raise efficiency by eliminating the pure tax component of PAYG contributions, it also would tend to reduce efficiency to the extent that it requires increased general taxation to

> **Box 3.4. Alternative Solutions to the Social Security Crisis**
>
> Recently, a number of authors have come forward with proposals to fundamentally reform the PAYG pension systems existing in most developed economies in ways that differ in at least some aspects from the World Bank's three-pillar model. For example:
>
> Modigliani (1999) puts forward a proposal to protect the FF system from market risk. His reform would preserve the *defined benefits* feature of the PAYG system by guaranteeing the real return on contributions. This would be achieved by pooling contributions and investing them in a single indexed portfolio consisting of an appropriate share of the market portfolio of publicly traded financial assets. The return of this portfolio would be "swapped" against that of a portfolio of treasury bonds carrying a guaranteed *real* rate of return (around 5 percent at the present time). This would limit the risk borne by individuals—such risk, he argues, is unacceptable for a compulsory savings plan—and shift to the government the risk that the return on the market portfolio may fall short of the guaranteed return. The government, he argues, is in a better position to absorb this risk because of its size and because, with infinite life, it can redistribute the risk of a single cohort over a large number of cohorts. Furthermore, it would allow the pension system to continue to play a redistributive role, which is extremely difficult under a defined contribution scheme. Such a scheme would also have the advantage of very low administrative costs, in contrast to management of individual portfolios.
>
> Others have suggested a move toward FF systems, but focused on the need for appropriate financing. Kotlikoff (1998) proposes a pension reform that replaces an existing PAYG system with an FF system, with transition costs financed by a consumption tax. Simulating such a pension reform with a calibrated model for the United States, Kotlikoff finds the pension reform to be welfare-improving across generations. However, the welfare effect does not stem from the pension reform itself, which imposes transition costs, but rather from the implicit tax reform that replaces a payroll tax with a consumption tax. Compared to a payroll tax, a consumption tax is associated with higher savings because individuals build additional savings to cover future consumption tax payments while keeping their intertemporal consumption profile constant.
>
> Sinn (1999) suggests prefunding of pensions by the current generation. The phenomenon of an aging society is the result of falling birth rates. Contrary to past generations, the present generation has not saved sufficiently for its retirement through raising children. Hence, mandating the present generation to save through an FF pillar in addition to existing PAYG schemes does not constitute an extra burden but rather can be viewed as a substitute to raising children.

pay for transition costs or for the interest payments on the higher explicit government debt. Further, it may not be necessary to reform the pension system to pursue particular economic objectives such as higher national saving; other measures, such as a move from direct to indirect taxes, could help achieve the same goals.

The benefits of higher average returns on contributions to the fully funded system come at the cost of exposing pensioners to higher investment risks. This is a potential major drawback since the primary objective of a pension system is to provide old-age security for workers. (As indicated in Table 3.2, replacement rates can vary dramatically with only moderate changes in average rates of return on FF investments.) The risks of the fully funded system can be particularly high in transition economies, given the low level of development of capital markets in these countries, especially if investments abroad by pension funds are limited by law (see below). Beyond normal investment risks, private pension funds could fall victim to fraud, in particular when financial sector regulation is still improving. Further, PAYG systems, with their benefits independent from the business cycle, can provide an element of insurance for the economy as a whole; PAYG proponents point to the depression of the 1930s as an example in which an FF system would have failed and led to even bigger economic contraction.

Private pension funds often generate high administrative costs—including for marketing—that are reflected in sizable administrative fees and charges. The share of social security contributions that goes to cover the insurance premia and the costs of running private pension funds in the countries that have introduced FF schemes total up to 4 percent of the fund's value annually. Such charges can have a large impact on the rate of return on pension investments. Similarly, in the absence of developed annuity markets, the higher returns of the second pillar relative to the PAYG implied returns may be eaten away by high discount rates for purchasing an annuity at retirement.

Options for Fully Funded Pillars in the Baltic Countries

All three countries have made substantial progress in moving to a three-pillar pension system. First, each has passed legislation establishing the legal

III INTRODUCTION OF A THREE-PILLAR PENSION SYSTEM

Table 3.2. Latvia: Retirement Scenarios in a Fully Funded System

	Annual Wage	Annual Contribution	Investment Performance			
			Stock Index (no cost)	Individuals		
				A	B	C
Wage replacement ratio[1]						
In retirement			31%	78%	26%	9%
Memorandum items:						
Assumptions (annual rates):						
Starting salary (currency)	1,800					
Wage growth	6%			6%	6%	6%
Contribution rate 2001–06		2%		2%	2%	2%
Contribution rate from 2007		10%		10%	10%	10%
Rate of return, gross			8%	12%	8%	4%
Annual cost, percent of NAV			0%	1%	1%	1%
Annual rate of return, net			8%	11%	7%	3%
			(In currency units)			
Buildup of assets and dis-saving during retirement						
2001	1,800	36	36	36	36	36
2002	1,908	38	77	78	77	75
2040	17,466	1,747	86,355	151,746	72,585	39,199
2041	18,514	1,851	95,114	170,290	79,517	42,226
2042	19,625	0	96,620	175,417	80,776	42,090
2043	20,803	0	97,880	180,241	81,829	41,839
2044	22,051	0	98,853	184,670	82,643	41,462
2045	23,374	0	99,492	188,599	83,177	40,946
2046	24,776	0	99,746	191,905	83,389	40,280
2047	26,263	0	99,558	194,449	83,232	39,449
2048	27,839	0	98,864	196,068	82,652	38,438
2049	29,509	0	97,596	196,579	81,592	37,231
2050	31,280	0	95,676	195,771	79,987	35,811
2051	33,156	0	93,018	193,402	77,765	34,160
2052	35,146	0	89,530	189,196	74,849	32,258
2053	37,254	0	85,106	182,841	71,150	30,084
2054	39,490	0	79,633	173,980	66,575	27,614
2055	41,859	0	72,985	162,208	61,018	24,826
2056	44,371	0	65,025	147,064	54,363	21,693
2057	47,033	0	55,600	128,026	46,483	18,186
2058	49,855	0	44,543	104,502	37,240	14,277
2059	52,846	0	31,671	75,822	26,479	9,934
2060	56,017	0	16,784	41,228	14,033	5,121
2061	59,378	0	–340	–139	–283	–196

Note: An individual works and contributes for 40 years, expects to be in retirement for 20 years.
Source: IMF staff estimates.
[1]Annual retirement benefit (wage replacement ratio) is calculated at a level to exhaust pension capital at the time of the expected death. The ratio is assumed to stay constant during retirement.

basis for operating the third, voluntary FF pillar, and this pillar is already in place in Latvia and Estonia. Second, in the mid-1990s all three countries, with assistance from the World Bank and other international advisors, developed detailed projections for the financing needs and operation of the mandatory FF pillar. However, progress in the actual creation of this pillar has been slow. Latvia, the most advanced in developing the second pillar, signed into law the main legislation defining the basic parameters of the second pillar in February 2000, and the mandatory FF pillar will start accepting contributions beginning July 2001. Estonia is also making progress in developing its second-pillar legislation and expects implementation to begin in 2001–02 as well. (Simulation results for different pension reform scenarios in Estonia are presented in the Appendix.) Lithuania, so far, has been moving more slowly than the other two Baltic states, although in April 2000 parliament approved a resolution asking the government to prepare a concept paper for reform of the old-age pension scheme beginning in 2002, along similar lines as its Baltic neighbors.

As the three countries move forward in implementing the three-tier system, they face a number of key decisions regarding the design of the fully funded pillar which will be crucial in determining the ultimate success of the reform. The following discussion examines the trade-offs involved in these decisions.

Size of the Pillars

The Baltic countries face the fundamental question of how to split payroll taxes between the first two pillars of the system. Most proponents of three-pillar systems would argue that a first pillar that is larger than necessary to provide a minimum safety net would be inefficient. However, the larger the first pillar remains, the lower the government's transition costs and the smaller the adverse impact on the transition generation.

Therefore, the size of the first pillar will depend to a considerable extent on the available sources of financing. It was in this context, in fact, that the Latvian government decided to limit contributions to the second tier scheme to 2 percent of salary, during the years 2001–06, gradually rising to no less than 4 percent in 2007, and to 10 percent from 2010 onwards.[26] In Estonia, the debate has focused on increasing the 20 percent social tax by 2 percentage points for participants of the FF pillar, while diverting 4 percent from the current social tax. This would ensure proper funding for the PAYG pillar, which would receive the remaining 16 percentage points of the social tax. While such limits on the size of the second pillar reduce the transition cost—in Estonia this cost is projected at about 1½ percent of GDP—so do they limit potential benefits of the reform.[27]

Financing the Transition to a Fully Funded System

The transitional deficit can be financed through either fiscal adjustment—some combination of higher taxes and reduced government spending—or increased debt. The first option—which, in effect, requires the prefunding of the current generation's pensions—would be expected in the long run to lead to higher savings. In fact, this effect can be seen as a primary benefit from the move to a three-pillar pension system (see Section IV). However, this option is likely to be met with political resistance from the transitional generation that is being forced to "pay twice" for pensions. Financing at least a portion of the deficit via borrowing (or, alternatively, using privatization receipts which otherwise would have been used to pay off existing debt) would help share the cost of transition between the present and future generations. However, financing via borrowing would not help tackle the demographic shift. While some of this borrowing may, in practice, come from surpluses generated in the private pension accounts over the medium term, taxes will have to increase to finance interest payments on the higher explicit debt. This higher taxation imposes a permanent efficiency cost offsetting, at least in part, the potential efficiency gains from the shift of labor from informal to the formal sector. Further, the accumulation of substantial explicit public sector debt could have an impact on confidence in the domestic economy, as reflected, for example, in the risk premium on foreign borrowing.

Participation in the Second Pillar

There are various possibilities regarding who should be included in the new system, and the extent to which individuals can choose to participate or not. At one extreme, some countries, such as Bolivia, Kazakhstan, and Mexico, have opted for a complete and mandatory shift from the old PAYG into the FF system. In most cases, however, the reforms provide for some level of choice especially to the middle-aged workers who have already accumulated substantial pension rights under the PAYG system.[28] The decision on who joins the FF pillar has strong bearings on the transition costs. For example, allowing only labor market entrants into the second pillar spreads out the transition costs over current and future generations to a maximum, thereby reducing the costs in any given year of the reform. However, in the absence of appropriate reforms to the first pillar, this would simply delay addressing the long-term solvency issue, at which the FF scheme is aimed.

In Latvia, the second tier scheme will be mandatory for all employees under 30 years old. Individuals subject to the state pension insurance and who

---

[26]The Law requires contributions to be "not less than 2 percent" during 2001–06.

[27]In Kazakhstan, by contrast, the second pillar receives 10 percentage points of the social tax, which has created tremendous pressure on the central government budget, and led to a reduction in existing real pension claims, via inflation.

[28]For a detailed review of typical switching options in pension reforms around the world and the switching decision process, see Palacios and Whitehouse (1998).

III INTRODUCTION OF A THREE-PILLAR PENSION SYSTEM

are age 30 to 49 when the Law takes effect in 2001 may affiliate with the FF scheme on a voluntary basis. For Estonia, it appears that participation in the second pillar could be mandatory for those under the age of 35 and optional for older workers. Under the current proposal, PAYG pensions would not be reduced significantly for those opting for the FF pillar, suggesting that a majority of Estonia workers will switch from the PAYG to the FF plan. A more careful design of incentives seems warranted to limit potential transition costs.

Administration of the Fully Funded System

An FF system can either be administered by a special class of licensed institutions (institutional pension funds), or can take the form of a special class of accounts or securities (individual pension accounts) that can be held with (or issued) by most licensed financial intermediaries. In a number of countries, the mandatory FF pillar is operated on the basis of individual pension accounts, administered by a single government-controlled or supervised provident fund. In more competitive environments, the FF pillar is operated by a number of specially licensed pension funds.[29] The most competitive environment is offered by systems where individual pension accounts can be opened with almost any financial intermediary, such as banking institutions, mutual funds (unit trusts), insurance companies, brokerages, and, conceivably, stock exchanges, or nonfinancial institutions.

The three Baltic countries still lack detailed regulations of the future second pillar. Estonia intends to allow 3–5 private pension funds to manage the investments of the second pillar, while the individual records would be monitored by a non-profit institution that could be financed by the treasury. In Latvia, it has been decided that the State Treasury will manage the accumulated resources in the mandatory pillar until January 1, 2003, but the institutional design beyond that date remains unclear. This may be sensible in the short run given the initial small size of the second pillar, as fixed administrative costs could be prohibitive with competing private firms. However, a move away from this setup would be needed over the medium-term to fully realize the expected benefits of an FF system. In particular, allowing the treasury to maintain control over pension resources would provide a potential captive source of government financing.[30] Both Estonia and Latvia are moving toward unified financial sector supervision, under which regulation of private pension funds would be incorporated.

Regulations on Investments Under the Second Pillar

Most countries impose investment guidelines for pension institutions. Some countries impose strict quantitative and qualitative restrictions while others require managers to follow prudent behavior. The former approach, common in continental Europe, has often been used to direct pension capital to specific types of investment, in particular domestic bonds issued by public institutions and domestic corporations. The latter approach, adopted by the United States, has forced managers to develop internal prudential rules, and is often credited with forcing U.S. managers to diversify outside the United States and into more varied investment instruments.

In this context, one of the key issues facing the Baltics is whether pension funds (or individual pension accounts) should be allowed to invest abroad. Allowing such investments would provide the opportunity to reduce portfolio risk and increase returns via diversification and would allow funds to hedge against country-specific shocks and risks. In this way, FF pensions can contribute to a solution to the demographic problem facing the Baltics. Further, investing abroad precludes pension funds from acquiring excessive market power in local capital markets and limits the extent to which pension funds become a source of "captive resources" for the government. Investment abroad is often prohibited, or limited, in part to maximize the potential impact of reform on the development of the domestic capital market. However, in the Baltics—small open economies fully integrated into world capital markets—this would appear to be a dubious objective. The Estonian authorities expect that the bulk of savings would be invested outside the country. Latvia has yet to make a decision on this point, but legislation for the third pillar limits investments abroad to 15 percent.

Operation Costs

Several options could help in lowering the administrative costs of a compulsory second pillar. One

---

[29]The government may determine who can establish a pension fund and under what conditions. Typically, employers, chambers of trade, professional associations, as well as employees' and/or employers' interest representation organizations, and government-run pension administration units are allowed to apply for licenses, provided they satisfy requirements, such as representing a certain minimum number of workers.

[30]In Kazakhstan, for example, the state pension accumulation fund—for those who did not opt for private funds—has largely purchased illiquid state securities.

possibility would be an employer-based second pillar similar to that in Switzerland, in which sponsors have a choice of in-house management, banks or insurance companies for the management of the pension plan (Queisser, 1999). Another option would be a centralized public institution, perhaps under the umbrella of the existing social security institution, with asset management provided through competing investment managers. Under such a model, the public institution would be able to negotiate asset management fees for all affiliates, while workers would still have a choice between investment portfolios; this option is currently being explored in the management of the Southeast Asian provident funds. A third option would have pensions invested in a broad international stock market index, which would imply extremely low administrative costs (Kotlikoff, 1999).

Risk Protection for Second Pillar Pensions

Institutional pension funds may offer some form of a guaranteed minimum rate of return on investments, underwritten by the government or a specially created insurance fund. While governments have generally not provided formal guarantees for possible second pillar losses, they may well end up bailing out failed private funds. In some cases (for example, Chile and Peru) risks are moderated by compensating the poorest performing pension funds out of the earnings of all pension funds. However, such guarantees should be avoided, as they can generate serious problems of moral hazard by encouraging overly risky investment decisions and raise administrative costs.

Beneficiaries of FF pensions may have several options for using their accumulated savings upon retirement. In the least restrictive regimes, individuals may have absolute freedom to withdraw all funds at a single time, spread the withdrawals as they wish, or simply pass on the funds to their heirs. Alternatively, beneficiaries may be given an option to withdraw some share of their saving in the FF account at any time after reaching a certain age, but require the purchase of an annuity with the remaining share, in order to ensure adequate retirement income and limit subsequent recourse to public assistance (Walliser, 1999). In more restrictive regimes, government regulations may require the purchase of specific annuities sold by licensed institutions; given the lack of developed annuity markets, such products may provide low rates of return to retirees (and high rents to the licensed institutions).

Tax Treatment of Pension Contributions and Benefits

Tax codes typically offer incentives to investors in both the mandatory and voluntary pension pillars. Tax benefits can be offered when investments are made, as earnings on invested savings accumulate, or at withdrawal. Specifically, income spent on periodic investments into the pension system can be deductible from taxable income for income tax purposes, or the pension capital can be allowed to accumulate tax-free until withdrawal, or the accumulated capital in the pension account can be withdrawn at retirement free of income taxes. The front-loaded incentives have an immediate and transparent budgetary cost and provide the most tangible immediate benefit to savers. The back-loaded incentives have a future and more uncertain fiscal cost, provide the highest potential benefit to savers who expect to have high retirement income, and may be seen as less credible by the public, who may not trust that future generations of politicians will honor these tax commitments. However, the back-loaded tax incentives are easier to administer because savers simply do not owe any taxes on the accumulated savings. Tax incentives may also be targeted to specific groups or purposes. For example, tax-free pension investments or withdrawals may be restricted to lower income groups, or access to pension savings before retirement could be limited to financing of health care or education expenses. This may be justified on the grounds that housing or educational expenditure in most instances offer an opportunity to diversify savings into nonfinancial assets or increase future earning potential. However, introducing such provisions complicates tax administration and can lead to significant revenue loss for the government.

IV   Macroeconomic Issues and Program Design

Pension System Reform and the Savings-Investment Balance

A pension reform that introduces an FF pillar or increases the importance of an existing FF pillar will affect the macroeconomic savings-investment balance in three basic ways. First, a tax-financed pension reform strengthens savings by substituting an FF pillar based on capital accumulation for a PAYG pillar based on intergenerational redistribution. Second, a pension reform involves transition costs that need to be financed; other things equal, this reduces national savings. Third, a pension reform can affect private savings outside the pension system.

This section focuses on the macroeconomic implications of a pension reform, in particular on its impact on private and aggregate savings. It is assumed throughout this section that the rate of return on FF savings is greater than the implicit rate of return on PAYG contributions.[31] As argued in Section III, this assumption should hold in the long run. However, this higher average rate of return is associated with a higher volatility. Two types of individual behavior are considered, one in which individuals are forward-looking, and a second in which they are myopic. Forward-looking individuals optimize an intertemporal preference function. Hence, their savings behavior is determined by their expected income, the rate of return, and the expected returns from the mandatory pension system. It is further assumed that Ricardian equivalence does not hold. Myopic individuals do not base their savings decision on intertemporal utility maximization.[32] Instead, savings are assumed to be based on a constant marginal propensity to save. Hence, myopic individuals can be expected to disregard some changes in lifetime income for their savings decision. Only changes in disposable income would lead to changes in savings, while changes in the rate of return leave savings unchanged. This case is quite relevant, since the existence of public pensions is based, in part, on the assumption that individuals are to a certain extent myopic.[33]

Individuals can use their private savings outside the mandatory pension system to adjust their pension savings in a utility-maximizing way. Prior to pension reform, individuals save for their retirement through a government-mandated pension system, funded by a payroll tax. In addition, individuals can accumulate private savings outside the pension system. If the government pension is perceived as too low, individuals build up additional savings to achieve a desired level of consumption during retirement.[34]

Individuals can also use private savings outside the pension system to react to an exogenous shock that leads to a fall in expected pension benefits. For example, an increase in the dependency ratio lowers PAYG pensions if the payroll tax and the replacement ratio are left unchanged because a smaller labor force has to provide for a larger number of pensioners. Demographic projections that show an increase in the dependency ratio over the next 30 years are readily available today. Forward-looking individuals who learn about this trend may increase their savings outside the pension system, since their expected PAYG pensions have declined. Myopic individuals, however, may not change their private savings behavior, since they may not adequately provide for retirement on a voluntary basis in the first place.

One option for governments concerned about future pension levels in the face of rising dependency ratios is to introduce a mandatory FF pillar alongside the existing PAYG pillar. Such "prefunding" would

---

[31]The return on FF savings equals the interest rate on long-term savings while the implicit return on PAYG contributions depends on the future dependency ratio, productivity growth, and the political process that sets the PAYG payroll tax and the pension benefit level.

[32]Myopic behavior as defined here does not include a discount rate which is considered "too high."

[33]Alternatively, seemingly myopic behavior could reflect the calculation that governments will step in to provide some minimum income level for individual retirees who do not save sufficiently.

[34]If the government pension is perceived as too high, an individual may borrow against future pension payments in capital markets.

require a rise in the payroll tax, with the additional pension contributions invested in an FF pillar. This payroll tax hike should optimally be set equal to the increase in private savings outside the pension system that would be accumulated by forward-looking individuals. Given that individuals behave, at least in part, myopically and therefore do not fully adjust their savings behavior outside the pension system, prefunding would imply a rise in aggregate savings and an improvement in the macroeconomic savings-investment balance.[35]

A policy considered in the Baltics would reduce the size of the existing PAYG pillar with the introduction of an FF pillar. The payroll tax would be left constant, with a reduced share going to the PAYG pillar, and the remainder going to the new FF pillar. This reduction in PAYG contributions leads, ceteris paribus, to a deficit in the PAYG pillar that needs to be financed. It should be noted that these transition costs result from the design of the PAYG system, under which the first generation receives a pension without having had to contribute to the system. Since the present value of contributions to and payments from the pension system over the life of its existence must be equal, the "last" generation—the reform generation—has, in effect, to pay for the first generation's pension, by providing a pension for the next-to-last generation (that is, current retirees) and for itself.[36]

Whether the PAYG pillar deficit is financed through fiscal adjustment or increased debt, the pension reform's impact on the savings-investment balance depends crucially on the adjustment of private savings outside the pension system.[37] This in turn depends on whether individuals behave more in a forward-looking way or more in a myopic way.[38]

A pension reform that is completely debt-financed and leaves the payroll tax constant will, if individuals are forward-looking, lead to a fall in private savings outside the pension system and in aggregate national savings.[39] The financing gap in the PAYG pillar is just equal to the new FF pillar savings because the reduction in the PAYG pillar contribution is equal to the FF pillar contribution. Hence, the savings balance of the pension system remains unchanged during the reform period. Therefore, any change in the aggregate savings-investment balance must stem from changes in private savings outside the pension system. Introducing an FF pillar while reducing the PAYG pillar increases the average return to the mandatory pension contributions because the FF pillar yields a higher return than the PAYG pillar. Thus, savings outside the pension system are reduced to allocate the gain in total income in a consumption-smoothing way over one's lifetime.[40, 41] If, however, individuals are myopic, the debt-financed pension reform leaves private savings outside the pension system as well as aggregate savings, constant.[42]

A pension reform that is completely payroll tax-financed, if individuals are forward-looking, leads to a fall in savings outside the pension system that just offsets the mandatory FF pillar savings, so that national savings are unchanged.[43] By raising the payroll tax by the full amount that is intended to go into the FF pillar, so that the PAYG pillar incurs no deficit, the government is, in effect, prefunding the existing PAYG pillar. Forward-looking individuals would, therefore, maintain their optimal intertemporal consumption profile, by reducing savings outside the system to the full extent that their mandatory pension savings rises. As there is also no deficit in the PAYG pillar, the macroeconomic savings-investment balance is not affected by the pension reform. If individuals are myopic, however, a payroll tax-financed pension reform would reduce their savings outside the pension system by less than the increase in mandatory FF pillar savings.[44] As there would be no attempt by myopic individuals to reestablish the optimal consumption path, savings would tend to fall only to the extent that the increased payroll tax lowers disposable income. Thus, aggregate savings rise in response to the pension reform, and the macroeconomic savings-investment balance improves.

---

[35]This assumes no labor supply response to the tax increase. Should the tax increase lead to a decline in formal labor market participation—which is not unlikely in the Baltics where payroll tax rates are already high—the impact on aggregate savings is not easily inferred. See Mackenzie, Gerson, and Cuevas (1997).

[36]Sinn (1999) shows that while these transition costs can be distributed over several generations through temporary debt-financing, the present value of the transition costs remains unchanged.

[37]Financing the deficit by selling government assets is equivalent to tax-financing since it amounts to a hidden tax. See below.

[38]A formal exposition of the following discussion is given in Schimmelpfennig (2000).

[39]Debt-financing of the pension reform cannot be turned into a Ponzi-scheme in which the outstanding debt including interest payments is rolled over from generation to generation. Eventually, the debt stock needs to be repaid. Sinn (1999) shows that this repayment is equivalent to the first generation's pension benefits.

[40]The riskiness of returns from FF pensions may also be higher, which might lead to an increase in precautionary savings.

[41]This line of reasoning assumes that there is only partial Ricardian equivalence. In the case of full Ricardian equivalence, debt-financing and tax-financing are equivalent in their macroeconomic impact. Full Ricardian equivalence is, however, based on very rigid assumptions that are commonly thought not to hold in the real world. For example, see Leiderman and Blejer (1987).

[42]This assumes that myopic individuals save a constant share of their disposable income. Since the pension reform leaves disposable income unchanged, private savings remain unchanged, too.

[43]The same would hold if the deficit is financed by a reduction in other government spending.

[44]Again assuming a constant savings rate out of disposable income.

IV MACROECONOMIC ISSUES AND PROGRAM DESIGN

If, as an alternative, the pension reform is financed by a consumption tax, national savings would be expected to rise. It is a well-known theoretical result that indirect taxation is associated with higher savings than direct taxation in a life-cycle framework. With indirect taxation, some of the taxes that have to be paid over an individual's lifetime fall due during retirement. Hence, savings are increased during one's working life to pay for these taxes during retirement, leaving the intertemporal consumption profile unchanged. The macroeconomic savings-investment balance should therefore improve if the pension reform is financed by a consumption tax. Kotlikoff (1998) shows that a pension reform that is financed by a consumption tax leads to an increase in aggregate savings. However, this effect does not result from the pension reform itself, but rather from the implied tax reform that substitutes indirect taxes for direct taxes.

To summarize, assuming that individuals are neither fully forward-looking nor fully myopic, a debt-financed pension reform leads to a fall in domestic savings, and a tax-financed pension reform leads to a rise in domestic savings. If, in addition, domestic investment is independent of domestic savings—as would likely be the case for small open economies such as the Baltics—the change in domestic savings translates directly to the savings-investment balance and thus the current account: A debt-financed pension reform leads to a deterioration of the current account, and a tax-financed pension reform leads to an improvement of the current account (see Table 4.1).

The issue of how best to finance a pension reform can therefore also be looked at from a macroeconomic management perspective.[45] A country with a strong current account position can rely relatively heavily on debt-financing, which allows for a distribution of the transition costs over many generations. A country with a weak current account position, however, should rely more on tax-financing to preserve external balance.

Implications of Pension Reform for Macroeconomic Policy Design

Several issues related to pension reform are relevant for macroeconomic policy design. First, the reform should seek to close any intertemporal PAYG financing gap. Second, fiscal accounts should allow this issue to be examined in a transparent fashion. Third, the financing of a pension reform should be appropriate in light of the country's macroeconomic position.[46]

Pension reforms are motivated in part by the need to close projected financing gaps over time in the PAYG system. While a PAYG system's intertemporal budget constraint (that is, that the present value of current and future revenues equals the present value of current and future expectations) can always be met if pension expenditures are determined by pension revenues, governments may target a pension benefit level and a payroll tax level that are not consistent given demographic trends and productivity growth, resulting in a potential financing gap. Moreover, the payroll tax required to achieve even a subsistence pension benefit level may be too high in the sense that it would lead to significant efforts at tax evasion and impose a heavy deadweight loss on the economy. A pension reform should then be judged, in part, on the basis of whether it closes the projected financing gap. The pension reform must produce a pension system that is able to deliver the pension benefits level targeted and promised by the government without undue strain on the economy.

The issues involved in pension system reform make clear that governments should report their accounts not only for the current period—on a cash-flow basis—but also on an accrual basis. Ideally, the sustainability of a pension reform would be analyzed in the context of an intertemporal budget constraint.[47] In light of this constraint, the current period fiscal stance can be analyzed with respect to how well it contributes to the intertemporal budgetary objectives. Of course, any long-term fiscal strategy must be based on viable short- and medium-run fiscal stances as well, in particular given the uncertainties associated with projecting long-run developments. In addition to ensuring consistency with the intertemporal budget constraint, each period's fiscal balance must be achievable in an orderly fashion, that is, any deficit must be financed without unsettling financial markets.

Financing a pension reform by borrowing amounts to making an implicit government debt explicit (see for example, Cangiano, Cottarelli, and Cubeddu, 1998). Under a PAYG system, the government promises current workers future pension benefits in return for their social security payroll tax contribution, incurring an implicit government debt. A pension reform that pays for the shortfall of PAYG contribu-

---

[45]For a somewhat different discussion of pension reform financing, see Holzmann (1998).

[46]The treatment of pension reforms in IMF programs is also addressed in International Monetary Fund (SM/97/108) and Heller (1998).

[47]Pension issues have been usefully addressed in the framework of intergenerational accounting. See, for example, Auerbach, Kotlikoff, and Leibfritz (1999).

Implications of Pension Reform for Macroeconomic Policy Design

Table 4.1. The Macroeconomic Impact of Pension Reform

	Forward-Looking Individuals	Imperfectly Forward-Looking Individuals	Myopic Individuals
Debt-Financed	Current account deteriorates.	Current account deteriorates.	Current account is unchanged.
Payroll Tax-Financed	Current account is unchanged.	Current account improves.	Current account improves.
Consumption Tax-Financed	Current account improves.	Current account improves.	Current account improves.

tions by issuing government debt makes this implicit government debt explicit, but does not increase the level of debt including contingent liabilities.

There may, however, be a recognition effect associated with moving from an implicit government debt to an explicit government debt. If international investors had not accounted for the implicit pension debt—perhaps reflecting the view that governments can more easily default on such debt—making it explicit could lead to a reassessment of the country's fundamentals. To counter such a recognition effect, international organizations such as the IMF should support a well-designed pension reform as a proper step toward intertemporal fiscal solvency and sound macroeconomic policies. EU accession countries should be commended for openly addressing any demographic challenge to their pension system.

Financing a pension reform by taxing amounts to a simple prefunding of an existing PAYG system, imposing a forced saving on current workers. To achieve a certain pension benefit level that exceeds the one provided by the PAYG system, the government requires workers to save. If this saving is channeled into an FF pillar within the social security system, government savings increase although, on an accrual basis, the effect on the government budget is zero.[48]

Financing a pension reform by using budget surpluses or one-time privatization proceeds amounts to levying a hidden tax.[49] If the budget surplus or the one-time privatization proceeds had not been used to finance the pension reform, they could have been passed on to workers through reduced taxes. Alternatively, they could have been used to pay down existing government debt. In this sense, financing a pension reform by using budget surpluses or one-time privatization proceeds increases government debt compared to the counterfactual, although it leaves it unchanged in an accounting sense. With respect to the pension budget, this way of financing also turns an implicit debt into an explicit debt.

The above analysis suggests that macroeconomic policy design should focus on the following issues:

- What is the size of the intertemporal budget gap, given the current policy stance and pension promises?

- Does the pension reform close the intertemporal budget gap?

- Is the short-run fiscal stance sustainable? If the pension reform is at least partly debt-financed, some fiscal consolidation may need to be programmed over the short and medium run to pay down the debt.

- Is the financing mix of the pension reform between taxes and debt appropriate given the country's current account and debt situation?

---

[48]Some authors (for example, Feldstein, 1998) hope that a pension reform may pay for itself if the rate of return in the FF pillar exceeds the PAYG return sufficiently and the tax increase needed to cover the transition costs is modest.

[49]This was suggested by Jenkins (1992) with respect to transition economies.

V Conclusions

The Baltic countries have made considerable effort during the course of the transition to ensure the long-term sustainability of their pension systems and the adequacy of retirement income. As described above, these efforts initially involved steps to shore up the pay-as-you-go system inherited from the Soviet period, including by reversing the early expansion of this system, increasing retirement ages to more sustainable levels, and linking more closely lifetime contributions and retirement benefits. While these steps met with some success in improving the financial health of the Baltic pension funds, gains were partially undone by subsequent ad hoc benefit increases. Further, the adverse demographic trends facing the Baltic countries led them to consider more fundamental pension reforms, in particular, the establishment of a three-pillar pension scheme, including a mandatory, fully funded, defined contribution second pillar.

While a move toward a fully funded pension system can potentially make an important contribution to the objectives of pension reform, such a change is neither necessary nor sufficient to meet these goals. As noted in the paper, the existing PAYG pension system can, at least in theory, be made sustainable by an appropriate adjustment of payroll tax rates and expected lifetime pension benefits, although the average replacement rate implied by such changes may well be fairly low, reflecting the expected demographic developments. The introduction of a fully funded pillar can help the Baltics address this demographic challenge only to the extent that this reform allows an increase in their long-term sustainable growth rates, either through their impact on savings and capital accumulation or by enhancing labor market efficiency. Whether this can be achieved will largely depend, in turn, on detailed decisions regarding the implementation of the second pillar, most of which remain to be made. Moreover, some benefits being pursued by the introduction of a fully funded scheme could also be pursued through other mechanisms; for example, a move from direct to indirect taxation could serve to increase private savings.

As the primary benefit of the introduction of a fully funded element to the pension system is the possibility of increased savings, the transition costs of this reform should be financed, to a substantial degree, by fiscal adjustment. The paper argues that the alternative of financing reform by increasing public sector debt is unlikely to generate additional savings for the economy and, as such, would not contribute to the objectives of pension reform. However, the prefunding implied by fiscal adjustment—either in the form of higher taxation or cuts in government spending—is likely to be a difficult political step, as it can be seen as imposing an inequitable burden on the current generation of workers. This difficulty has undoubtedly influenced the decisions of both Latvia and Estonia to begin with a rather small second pillar, limiting both the potential costs and benefits of the reform.

The paper has a number of other implications for the optimal design and implementation of a fully funded pension pillar in the Baltics, including that:

- Given the need to generate adequate returns on pension fund investments and encourage risk diversification, any fully funded pension should be allowed to invest abroad. Given that the Baltics are small open economies with access to international capital markets, attempting to stimulate domestic capital markets through tight limits on investment abroad is unnecessary and could well be counterproductive.

- Any guarantees—implicit or explicit—on the returns of individual pension funds or accounts should be strongly resisted as they would introduce potentially severe problems of moral hazard and raise administrative costs. Regulation of pension funds or accounts should focus primarily on ensuring transparency in operations and full disclosure.

- Indexation should allow retirees to partially share in the expected sizable productivity gains in the Baltics over the medium term, allowing both real increases in retirement income and a decline in the first pillar deficit. Both Latvia's gradual move from CPI indexation to wage indexation, as well as Estonia's proposal to index

Conclusions

to a weighted average of the wage fund and CPI, would appear to meet these objectives.

Finally, the success of the three-pillar scheme will also depend on the ability of the three countries to continue to strengthen the long-term finances of the pay-as-you-go pillar. Key steps in this regard will include increasing the retirement age over time and resisting future pressures for unsustainable increases in benefits.

References

Auerbach, Alan, Laurence J. Kotlikoff, and Willi Leibfritz, editors, 1999, *Generational Accounting Around the World* (Chicago: University of Chicago Press).

Brooks, Robin, 2000, "What Will Happen to Financial Markets When the Baby Boomers Retire?" IMF Working Paper 00/18 (Washington: International Monetary Fund).

Cangiano, Marco, Carlo Cottarelli, and Luis Cubeddu, 1998, "Pension Developments and Reforms in Transition Economies," IMF Working Paper 98/151 (Washington: International Monetary Fund).

Central Statistics Bureau of Latvia, *1998 Statistical Yearbook of Latvia* (Riga).

Federal Reserve Board, 1997, "Family Finances in the U.S.: Recent Evidence from the Survey of Consumer Finances," *Federal Reserve Bulletin,* Vol. 83, No. 1.

Feldstein, Martin, 1998, *Privatizing Social Security* (Chicago and London: University of Chicago Press).

Fox, Louise, 1998, "Pension Reform in the Post-Communist Transition Economies," *Transforming Post-Communist Political Economies,* ed. by Joan Nelson, Charles Tilly, and Lee Walker (Washington: National Research Council).

Fox, Louise, and Edward Palmer, 1999, *Latvian Pension Reform* (Washington: World Bank).

Gassmann, Franziska, 2000, "Who and Where are Poor in Latvia" (Riga: Ministry of Welfare of the Republic of Latvia).

Heller, Peter S., 1998, "Rethinking Public Pension Reform Initiatives," IMF Working Paper 98/61 (Washington: International Monetary Fund).

Hemming, Richard, 1998, "Should Public Pensions be Funded?" IMF Working Paper 98/35 (Washington: International Monetary Fund).

Holzmann, Robert, 1998, *Financing the Transition (*Washington: World Bank mimeo).

International Monetary Fund, 1997, *Assessing the Fiscal Stance in the Context of Privatizing a Public Pension System,* SM/97/108 (Washington: International Monetary Fund).

Jenkins, Glenn, 1992, "Privatization and Pension Reform in Transition Economies," *Public Finance*, Vol. 47. Supplement, pp. 141–151.

Kotlikoff, Laurence J., 1998, "The A–K Model—Its Past, Present, and Future," NBER Working Paper 6684 (Cambridge, Massachusetts: National Bureau of Economic Research). http://www.nber.org/papers/w6684

———, 1999, "The World Bank's Approach and the Right Approach to Reforming Social Security." http://econ.bu.edu/faculty/kotlikoff/adb.pdf

Leiderman, Leozada and Mario Blejer, 1987, "Modeling and Testing Ricardian Equivalence: A Survey," IMF Working Paper 87/35 (Washington: International Monetary Fund).

Mackenzie, George and Philip Gerson and Alfredo Cuevas, 1997, *Pension Regimes and Savings*, IMF Occasional Paper No. 153 (Washington: International Monetary Fund).

Ministry of Welfare of the Republic of Latvia, 1999, *Who and Where Are Poor in Latvia (*Riga).

Ministry of Welfare of the Republic of Latvia, 1999, *New indexation—Rules from the Year 2000.* (Riga).

Ministry of Welfare of the Republic of Latvia, 1999, *Pension Reform in Latvia* (Riga).

Modigliani, Franco, Maria Luisa Ceprini, and Arun Muralidhar, "A Solution to the Social Security Crisis," Sloan Working Paper No. 4051 (Cambridge, Massachusetts: Massachusetts Institute of Technology).

Palacios, Robert, and Edward Whitehouse, 1998, "The Role of Choice in the Transition to a Funded Pension System," Social Protection Discussion Paper No. 9812 (Washington: World Bank).

Queisser, Monika, 1998, "Pension Reform: Lessons from Latin America," OECD Policy Brief No. 15 (Paris: OECD).

Schimmelpfennig, A., 2000, "Pension Reform, Private Savings, and the Current Account in a Small Open Economy," IMF Working Paper 00/171 (Washington: International Monetary Fund).

Sinn, Hans-Werner, 1999, "The Crisis in Germany's Pension Insurance System and How it Can Be Solved" (unpublished).

Sinn, Hans-Werner, 2000, "Why a Funded Pension System is Useful and Why It is Not Useful," NBER Working Paper 7592 (Cambridge, Massachusetts: National Bureau of Economic Research).

United States, Social Security Administration, 1997, *Social Security Bulletin*, Vol. 60, No. 1, International Updates (Washington).

———, Social Security History, see website *www.ssa.gov/history/history6.html*

Walliser, Jan, 1999, "Regulations of Withdrawals in Individual Account Systems," IMF Working Paper 99/153 (Washington: International Monetary Fund).

World Bank, 1998, *Lithuania: An Opportunity for Economic Success* (Washington: World Bank).

World Bank, 1994, *Averting the Old Age Crisis* (New York, Oxford University Press).

World Bank Pensions Primer—Notes, Papers, Country and Regional Studies, Issues in Pension Reform. See Pension Primer on the World Bank website: *www.worldbank.org.*

Appendix. Estonia: Pension Reform[1]

Over the next 30 to 50 years, the structure of the Estonian population will change dramatically (Figure A.1). Low fertility could cause the total population to decline, while decreasing mortality will increase the number of elderly. The share of the population that is 65 years of age or more is projected to roughly double, from 15 percent of the population in 2000 to almost 30 percent in 2050. Concomitantly, the old-age dependency rate—defined as the ratio of people 65 and over to the working-age (aged 15 to 64) population—will more than double, from 20 percent to 50 percent. To address these trends before they create severe financial stress on the pension system, the authorities have adopted a two-pronged reform strategy. First, the parameters and administration of the current pay-as-you-go system are being carefully reviewed and, where appropriate, adjusted. The authorities are also considering a new provision for the indexation of both new and existing pensions. Second, the government is considering a funded pension pillar, whereby a portion of pension contributions would be redirected into individual retirement savings accounts. This would be in addition to a third, voluntary funded pillar already in place for which tax incentives are given.

The Framework for Pension Reform

The first step in the reform of the pension system was the introduction in 1994 of a plan to increase the retirement ages for both men and women. Under a revised and accelerated schedule, the retirement age will also be unified at 63, with men reaching the target age in 2001. The retirement age for women will increase more gradually, reaching 63 in 2016. The next step was the preparation in 1997 by the newly established Social Insurance Reform Committee of a "Conceptual Framework for Pension Reform." This paper identified the problems with the then-current system and laid out an overall reform strategy, including adjustments to the pay-as-you-go pillar, introduction of a funded, second pillar, and the establishment of the necessary institutional structure to support these reforms.

Pay-as-you-go pillar. The "Conceptual Framework" identified several problems with the pay-as-you-go pillar, including:

- the unfavorable demographic trends;

- easy access to the system, including a low retirement age, and loose eligibility requirements for disability pensions, and an array of pensions granted on favorable terms;

- various conditions under which participants received credit toward a pension without making contributions;

- social tax evasion;

- increasing participation in the shadow economy; and

- unintended redistribution.

Thus far, these problems have been addressed in a piecemeal fashion. In addition to the phased increase in retirement ages, the conditions for obtaining disability and special pensions have been tightened, and the definition of noncontributory service has been narrowed. To improve compliance, the responsibility for collecting social-insurance contributions has been shifted from the Pension Fund to the Tax Board. A new formula for benefits was introduced that provides a (somewhat tenuous) link between contributions and benefits. Finally, to support the new benefit formula, a Central Securities Depository has been established to maintain individual records and serve as an intermediary for the proposed second pillar. The likely effects of these changes on the finances of the pay-as-you-go pillar are examined here and possible options for addressing the problems identified in the "Conceptual Framework" are suggested.

Funded, defined-contribution pillar. A variety of reasons have been offered for the introduction of a

---
[1]The Appendix is based on the work of a Fiscal Affairs Department mission on pension reform headed by Mr. Gillingham. The authorities have agreed to the use of the materials contained in the technical assistance report.

APPENDIX

funded, defined-contribution pillar. Some relate to its direct effect on the pension system, including:

- the opportunity to benefit from investment in financial markets, where the rate of return is likely to be higher than the implicit rate of return to contributions in a pay-as-you-go pension system;
- a more individual focus, which can make retirement saving more transparent and improve compliance incentives; and
- a reduction in the vulnerability of the pension system to adverse demographic trends and political pressures.

In addition, it has been suggested that a shift to at least partial funding will provide additional capital to spur economic growth and contribute to the deepening of capital markets. These macroeconomic justifications are problematic. First, fully funded pension schemes are subject to the same rate of return risk from demographic developments as pay-as-you-go schemes. Second, the increase in private retirement saving may be offset—in full or in part—by a reduction in other private and government saving, although the offset can be limited by a prudent fiscal stance that limits the reduction in public saving.[2] Moreover, it is not necessary to reform the pension system to pursue the goal of increased national saving. Finally, the presumed deepening of capital markets is likely to be of limited value in a small, open economy such as Estonia. Consequently, this appendix focuses on the direct implications of a funded pillar on the pension system.

The primary impediment to the introduction of a funded pillar are the transition costs that are generated. Redirecting pension contributions from the current pay-as-you-go system to funded individual accounts will reduce revenues in the short and medium term without reducing benefits. This problem has been at the forefront of the authorities' deliberations. The goal is to effect the transition without increasing the social-insurance contribution rate. Consequently, the trade-off is stark: the smaller the share of contributions redirected to the second pillar, the lower the benefits of funding; the higher the share, the greater the financing gap in the pay-as-you-go pillar. A plan currently under consideration is to shift 4 percentage points of the current contribution rate to the second pillar, while requiring participants in the second pillar to pay an additional 2 percentage points. This appendix evaluates the implications of this proposal and presents alternative structures.

---

[2]See Mackenzie, Gerson, and Cuevas (1997).

Summary of Findings

Macroeconomic and Demographic Setting

Estonia's conditions for pension reform are positive. Strong growth is likely to continue over the next several years, and longer to the extent that productivity—and wages—in Estonia converge to levels in more advanced economies (the base case assumes that wages will converge to the average level in the European Union over 75 years). Long-term demographic trends heighten the need for pension reform. Population in Estonia is projected to fall at an average annual rate of 0.3 percent over the next 30 years, curtailing the growth of aggregate pension contributions, just as population aging and decreasing mortality add to the number of pensioners. These adverse trends provide the motivation for the authorities' proposal to introduce a funded pension pillar. However, it is important to note that medium-term population trends are more favorable. The ratio of contributors to beneficiaries is projected to grow over the next decade, and to stay above the current level of 1.7 for almost 20 years. This provides a window for pension reform to proceed at an orderly pace.

Pay-As-You-Go Pillar

The essential dilemma in reforming the pay-as-you-go pillar is to balance the desire to maintain replacement rates—defined here as the average benefit as a percentage of the average wage gross of tax—against the requirement for financial integrity.[3] For this reason, the key assumption in the base case for simulating pension reform options is that new and existing pensions will be indexed with a simple average of the rate of increase in the CPI and wages subject to contributions. This index—which is the preferred indexation option of the Social Insurance Reform Committee—strikes a compromise between the desires to limit increases without reducing real benefits (the CPI) and to allow pensioners to share the benefits of increasing aggregate wages (the wage fund). Under the assumptions of this base-case scenario (Figures A.1 and A.2):

- the first pillar runs consistent and large surpluses, which average over 1 percent of GDP over the projection period (2001–75), and

---

[3]Although we measure replacement rates with respect to before-tax income, it is important to remember that labor income over EEK 800 is subject to a 26 percent marginal income tax rate while pensions are not taxed. Consequently, the rate of replacement of after-tax income is substantially higher (currently approximately 47 percent).

APPENDIX

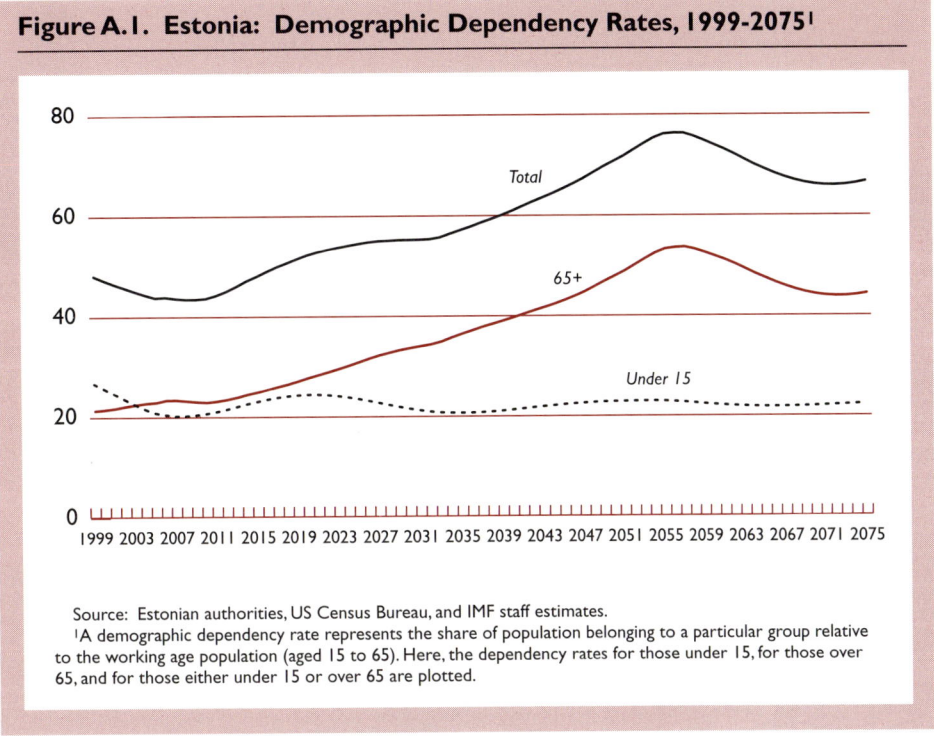

Figure A.1. Estonia: Demographic Dependency Rates, 1999-2075[1]

Source: Estonian authorities, US Census Bureau, and IMF staff estimates.
[1] A demographic dependency rate represents the share of population belonging to a particular group relative to the working age population (aged 15 to 65). Here, the dependency rates for those under 15, for those over 65, and for those either under 15 or over 65 are plotted.

- the replacement rate falls dramatically, from 38 percent to 17 percent by 2050.

This scenario implies that, all other things equal, there is room to increase future replacement rates without pushing the system into insolvency. To demonstrate this, an alternative scenario increases the weight of the wage fund in the index used to adjust pensions from one half to two-thirds. This scenario yielded:

- a zero average balance over the projection period, and
- a modest improvement in future replacement rates over the base scenario.

This second scenario demonstrates how difficult it would be to curtail the fall in replacement rates using the same index to adjust both new and existing pensions. Following practice in many countries, the third simulation holds the replacement rate for new pensions constant and indexes subsequent benefits with the CPI. Under this scenario, benefits are cut for current retirees and those workers who will retire in the near future, but increased for younger workers. Although this scenario runs surpluses over the mid term as benefits are reduced, holding the initial replacement rate constant in the face of an increasing dependency rate eventually drives the system into continuing deficits that average roughly 1 percent of GDP. After an initial fall as a result of the new indexation rule, the average replacement rate stabilizes at approximately 25 percent.

In an attempt to curtail the increase in the dependency ratio, the final simulation assumed that the pending increase in the retirement age for women would be accelerated, and the retirement ages for both men and women would be increased to 65 by 2025. This scenario cuts future benefits relative to the baseline and yields somewhat lower deficits.

These simulations demonstrate how difficult it is to maintain replacement rates in the pay-as-you-go pillar simply by adjusting the parameters of the system. This conclusion is the impetus behind the authorities' proposal to implement a funded second pillar.

Second Pillar

As noted above, the attempt to implement a second pillar faces a stark trade-off between the share of contributions that can be redirected to the second pillar and the financing gap this creates. The base case for analyzing second-pillar alternatives is the option to redirect 4 percentage points of the current contribution rate to the funded pillar. The assumption was that workers 35 years of age and younger

APPENDIX

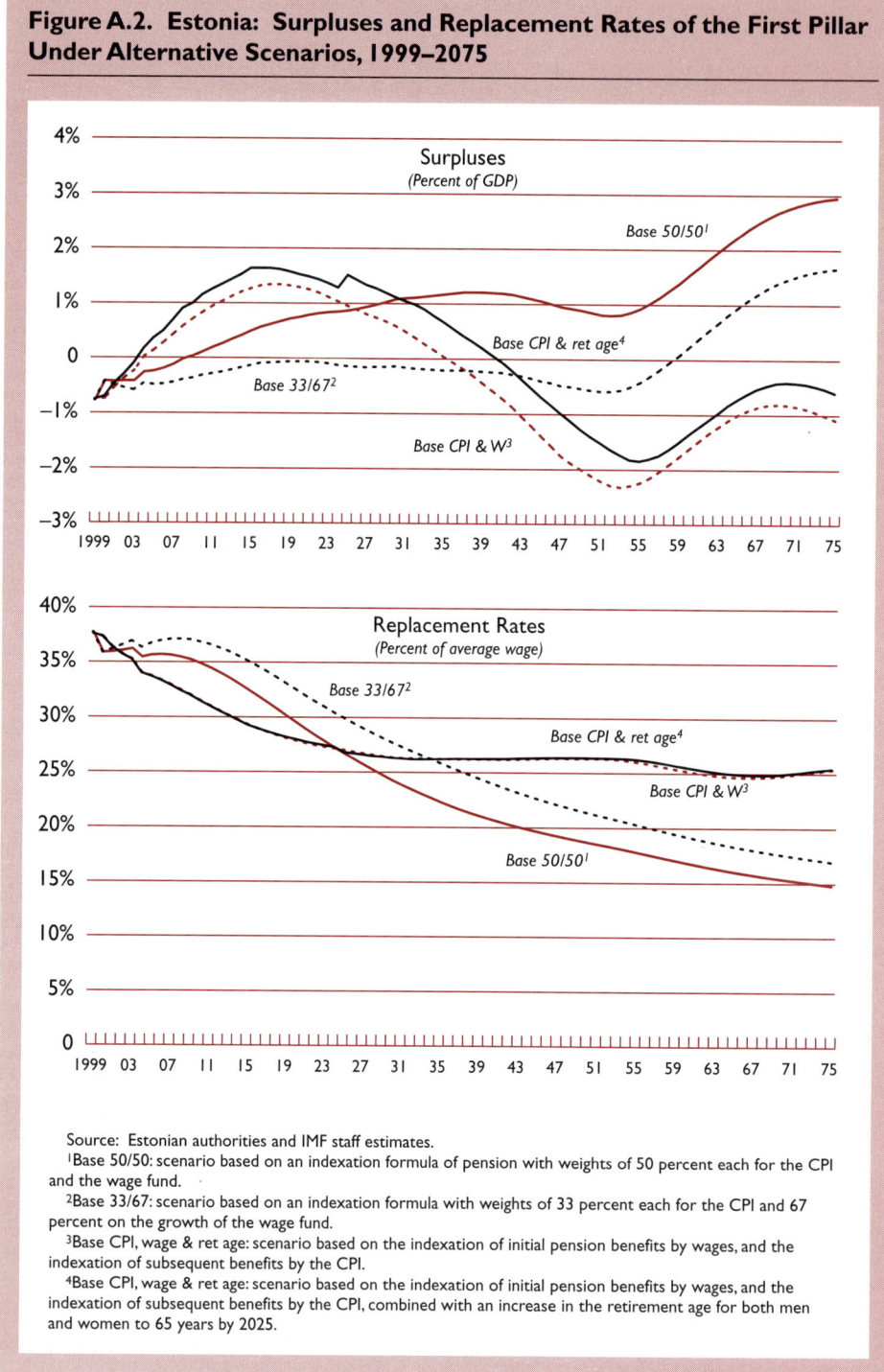

Figure A.2. Estonia: Surpluses and Replacement Rates of the First Pillar Under Alternative Scenarios, 1999–2075

Source: Estonian authorities and IMF staff estimates.
[1] Base 50/50: scenario based on an indexation formula of pension with weights of 50 percent each for the CPI and the wage fund.
[2] Base 33/67: scenario based on an indexation formula with weights of 33 percent each for the CPI and 67 percent on the growth of the wage fund.
[3] Base CPI, wage & ret age: scenario based on the indexation of initial pension benefits by wages, and the indexation of subsequent benefits by the CPI.
[4] Base CPI, wage & ret age: scenario based on the indexation of initial pension benefits by wages, and the indexation of subsequent benefits by the CPI, combined with an increase in the retirement age for both men and women to 65 years by 2025.

would be required to switch to the new system, and older workers would be given the option to switch. First-pillar benefits are assumed to be indexed to the same simple average of increases in the CPI and wage fund used in the base-case scenario for the first-pillar simulations. Under this scenario:

- the initial financing gap in the first-pillar averages over 1 percent of GDP per year for the first 12 years;

- over the remaining years, first pillar gradually recovers, and by the end of the projection period is generating surpluses of about 2 percent of GDP; and

- the funded pillar allows replacement rates to be higher for future workers, for instance reaching 25.5 percent in 2050 as compared to 17 percent without the second pillar.

If the initial financing gap, which peaks at 1.5 percent of GDP in 2005, creates too great a strain on the budget, it is possible to delay the transition costs by reducing the flow of workers into the second pillar. The second scenario assumes workers 25 and under would be required to switch and are the only ones who can. Under this scenario, the transition costs are spread out more smoothly into the future, averaging 0.2 percent of GDP during the years prior to 2055, when the system starts running surpluses.

Finally, there is general agreement that it would be preferable to divert more than 4 percentage points of pension contributions to the funded pillar, except for the transition costs that would be incurred. The delayed eligibility in the previous simulation facilitates the adoption of a more aggressive policy. The final second-pillar simulation redirects 6 percentage points to the funded pillar. Although it runs larger initial deficits—an average of 0.75 percent over the first 50 years—it too yields surpluses in the latter years of the simulation period.

An important lesson of the second-pillar simulations is that even if a policy causes first-pillar deficits in the early years, the current balance in each turns positive by 2060. In addition, they allow higher replacement rates for later cohorts than do the first-pillar reforms simulated here. Moreover, the improving balances in the later years of the simulation imply that additional resources might be shifted to the second pillar in the future.

Rate of return risk in the funded pillar. The expected benefits of the second pillar stem from the portfolio diversification they allow. The higher return is obtained at the cost of increased risk, however. A simulation of the replacement rates that could be supported by actual return sequences in the U.S. stock market demonstrates this risk. The expected replacement rates are very high, but so are the risks.

Institutional infrastructure. The authorities have established a number of institutions and a regulatory setting that should be conducive to the efficient operation of the second pillar. Collection of social security contributions has already been shifted to the Tax Board, and the institutions to maintain individual records have been established to enable the shift to contributions-based benefits. These steps should keep transaction costs to a minimum. The government intends to allow international portfolio diversification.

Recent Occasional Papers of the International Monetary Fund

200. Pension Reform in the Baltics: Issues and Prospects, by Jerald Schiff, Niko Hobdari, Axel Schimmelpfennig, and Roman Zytek. 2000.

199. Ghana: Economic Development in a Democratic Environment, by Sérgio Pereira Leite, Anthony Pellechio, Luisa Zanforlin, Girma Begashaw, Stefania Fabrizio, and Joachim Harnack. 2000.

198. Setting Up Treasuries in the Baltics, Russia, and Other Countries of the Former Soviet Union: An Assessment of IMF Technical Assistance, by Barry H. Potter and Jack Diamond. 2000.

197. Deposit Insurance: Actual and Good Practices, by Gillian G.H. Garcia. 2000.

196. Trade and Trade Policies in Eastern and Southern Africa, by a staff team led by Arvind Subramanian, with Enrique Gelbard, Richard Harmsen, Katrin Elborgh-Woytek, and Piroska Nagy. 2000.

195. The Eastern Caribbean Currency Union—Institutions, Performance, and Policy Issues, by Frits van Beek, José Roberto Rosales, Mayra Zermeño, Ruby Randall, and Jorge Shepherd. 2000.

194. Fiscal and Macroeconomic Impact of Privatization, by Jeffrey Davis, Rolando Ossowski, Thomas Richardson, and Steven Barnett. 2000.

193. Exchange Rate Regimes in an Increasingly Integrated World Economy, by Michael Mussa, Paul Masson, Alexander Swoboda, Esteban Jadresic, Paolo Mauro, and Andy Berg. 2000.

192. Macroprudential Indicators of Financial System Soundness, by a staff team led by Owen Evans, Alfredo M. Leone, Mahinder Gill, and Paul Hilbers. 2000.

191. Social Issues in IMF-Supported Programs, by Sanjeev Gupta, Louis Dicks-Mireaux, Ritha Khemani, Calvin McDonald, and Marijn Verhoeven. 2000.

190. Capital Controls: Country Experiences with Their Use and Liberalization, by Akira Ariyoshi, Karl Habermeier, Bernard Laurens, Inci Ötker-Robe, Jorge Iván Canales Kriljenko, and Andrei Kirilenko. 2000.

189. Current Account and External Sustainability in the Baltics, Russia, and Other Countries of the Former Soviet Union, by Donal McGettigan. 2000.

188. Financial Sector Crisis and Restructuring: Lessons from Asia, by Carl-Johan Lindgren, Tomás J.T. Baliño, Charles Enoch, Anne-Marie Gulde, Marc Quintyn, and Leslie Teo. 1999.

187. Philippines: Toward Sustainable and Rapid Growth, Recent Developments and the Agenda Ahead, by Markus Rodlauer, Prakash Loungani, Vivek Arora, Charalambos Christofides, Enrique G. De la Piedra, Piyabha Kongsamut, Kristina Kostial, Victoria Summers, and Athanasios Vamvakidis. 2000.

186. Anticipating Balance of Payments Crises: The Role of Early Warning Systems, by Andrew Berg, Eduardo Borensztein, Gian Maria Milesi-Ferretti, and Catherine Pattillo. 1999.

185. Oman Beyond the Oil Horizon: Policies Toward Sustainable Growth, edited by Ahsan Mansur and Volker Treichel. 1999.

184. Growth Experience in Transition Countries, 1990–98, by Oleh Havrylyshyn, Thomas Wolf, Julian Berengaut, Marta Castello-Branco, Ron van Rooden, and Valerie Mercer-Blackman. 1999.

183. Economic Reforms in Kazakhstan, Kyrgyz Republic, Tajikistan, Turkmenistan, and Uzbekistan, by Emine Gürgen, Harry Snoek, Jon Craig, Jimmy McHugh, Ivailo Izvorski, and Ron van Rooden. 1999.

182. Tax Reform in the Baltics, Russia, and Other Countries of the Former Soviet Union, by a staff team led by Liam Ebrill and Oleh Havrylyshyn. 1999.

181. The Netherlands: Transforming a Market Economy, by C. Maxwell Watson, Bas B. Bakker, Jan Kees Martijn, and Ioannis Halikias. 1999.

180. Revenue Implications of Trade Liberalization, by Liam Ebrill, Janet Stotsky, and Reint Gropp. 1999.

179. Dinsinflation in Transition: 1993–97, by Carlo Cottarelli and Peter Doyle. 1999.

178. IMF-Supported Programs in Indonesia, Korea, and Thailand: A Preliminary Assessment, by Timothy Lane, Atish Ghosh, Javier Hamann, Steven Phillips, Marianne Schulze-Ghattas, and Tsidi Tsikata. 1999.

177. Perspectives on Regional Unemployment in Europe, by Paolo Mauro, Eswar Prasad, and Antonio Spilimbergo. 1999.

176. Back to the Future: Postwar Reconstruction and Stabilization in Lebanon, edited by Sena Eken and Thomas Helbling. 1999.

175. Macroeconomic Developments in the Baltics, Russia, and Other Countries of the Former Soviet Union, 1992–97, by Luis M. Valdivieso. 1998.

174. Impact of EMU on Selected Non–European Union Countries, by R. Feldman, K. Nashashibi, R. Nord, P. Allum, D. Desruelle, K. Enders, R. Kahn, and H. Temprano-Arroyo. 1998.

173. The Baltic Countries: From Economic Stabilization to EU Accession, by Julian Berengaut, Augusto Lopez-Claros, Françoise Le Gall, Dennis Jones, Richard Stern, Ann-Margret Westin, Effie Psalida, Pietro Garibaldi. 1998.

172. Capital Account Liberalization: Theoretical and Practical Aspects, by a staff team led by Barry Eichengreen and Michael Mussa, with Giovanni Dell'Ariccia, Enrica Detragiache, Gian Maria Milesi-Ferretti, and Andrew Tweedie. 1998.

171. Monetary Policy in Dollarized Economies, by Tomás Baliño, Adam Bennett, and Eduardo Borensztein. 1998.

170. The West African Economic and Monetary Union: Recent Developments and Policy Issues, by a staff team led by Ernesto Hernández-Catá and comprising Christian A. François, Paul Masson, Pascal Bouvier, Patrick Peroz, Dominique Desruelle, and Athanasios Vamvakidis. 1998.

169. Financial Sector Development in Sub-Saharan African Countries, by Hassanali Mehran, Piero Ugolini, Jean Phillipe Briffaux, George Iden, Tonny Lybek, Stephen Swaray, and Peter Hayward. 1998.

168. Exit Strategies: Policy Options for Countries Seeking Greater Exchange Rate Flexibility, by a staff team led by Barry Eichengreen and Paul Masson with Hugh Bredenkamp, Barry Johnston, Javier Hamann, Esteban Jadresic, and Inci Ötker. 1998.

167. Exchange Rate Assessment: Extensions of the Macroeconomic Balance Approach, edited by Peter Isard and Hamid Faruqee. 1998

166. Hedge Funds and Financial Market Dynamics, by a staff team led by Barry Eichengreen and Donald Mathieson with Bankim Chadha, Anne Jansen, Laura Kodres, and Sunil Sharma. 1998.

165. Algeria: Stabilization and Transition to the Market, by Karim Nashashibi, Patricia Alonso-Gamo, Stefania Bazzoni, Alain Féler, Nicole Laframboise, and Sebastian Paris Horvitz. 1998.

164. MULTIMOD Mark III: The Core Dynamic and Steady-State Model, by Douglas Laxton, Peter Isard, Hamid Faruqee, Eswar Prasad, and Bart Turtelboom. 1998.

163. Egypt: Beyond Stabilization, Toward a Dynamic Market Economy, by a staff team led by Howard Handy. 1998.

162. Fiscal Policy Rules, by George Kopits and Steven Symansky. 1998.

161. The Nordic Banking Crises: Pitfalls in Financial Liberalization? by Burkhard Drees and Ceyla Pazarbaşıoğlu. 1998.

160. Fiscal Reform in Low-Income Countries: Experience Under IMF-Supported Programs, by a staff team led by George T. Abed and comprising Liam Ebrill, Sanjeev Gupta, Benedict Clements, Ronald McMorran, Anthony Pellechio, Jerald Schiff, and Marijn Verhoeven. 1998.

159. Hungary: Economic Policies for Sustainable Growth, Carlo Cottarelli, Thomas Krueger, Reza Moghadam, Perry Perone, Edgardo Ruggiero, and Rachel van Elkan. 1998.

158. Transparency in Government Operations, by George Kopits and Jon Craig. 1998.

157. Central Bank Reforms in the Baltics, Russia, and the Other Countries of the Former Soviet Union, by a staff team led by Malcolm Knight and comprising Susana Almuiña, John Dalton, Inci Otker, Ceyla Pazarbaşıoğlu, Arne B. Petersen, Peter Quirk, Nicholas M. Roberts, Gabriel Sensenbrenner, and Jan Willem van der Vossen. 1997.

156. The ESAF at Ten Years: Economic Adjustment and Reform in Low-Income Countries, by the staff of the International Monetary Fund. 1997.

Note: For information on the title and availability of Occasional Papers not listed, please consult the IMF Publications Catalog or contact IMF Publication Services.